Tales of a First-Round Nothing

* My Life as an NHL Footnote

Terry Ryan

ecw press

Published by ECW Press
2120 Queen Street East, Suite 200
Toronto, Ontario, Canada M4E 1E2
416-694-3348 / info@ecwpress.com

LIBRARY AND ARCHIVES CANADA CATALOGUING IN PUBLICATION

Ryan, Terry, 1977–, author
Tales of a first-round nothing : my life as an NHL footnote / Terry Ryan.

ISBN: 978-1-77041-139-5 (PBK.)
ALSO ISSUED AS: 978-1-77090-504-7 (EPUB); 978-1-77090-503-0 (PDF)

1. Ryan, Terry, 1977–. 2. Hockey players—Canada—Biography.
3. Montreal Canadiens (Hockey team)—Biography.

I. Title.
GV848.5.R93A3 2014 796.962092 C2013-907763-4 C2013-907764-2

Editor for the press: Michael Holmes
Cover design: David Gee
Cover photo courtesy of the author
Back cover photo: © Brian Tuck
Interior images courtesy of Terry Ryan, except where otherwise credited.
Photo section: Lynn Gammie
Text design and typesetting: Lynn Gammie
Printing: United Graphics 5 4 3

The publication of *Tales of a First-Round Nothing* has been generously supported by the Canada Council for the Arts which last year invested $157 million to bring the arts to Canadians throughout the country, and by the Ontario Arts Council (OAC), an agency of the Government of Ontario, which last year funded 1,681 individual artists and 1,125 organizations in 216 communities across Ontario for a total of $52.8 million. We also acknowledge the financial support of the Government of Canada through the Canada Book Fund for our publishing activities, and the contribution of the Government of Ontario through the Ontario Book Publishing Tax Credit and the Ontario Media Development Corporation.

PRINTED AND BOUND IN THE UNITED STATES

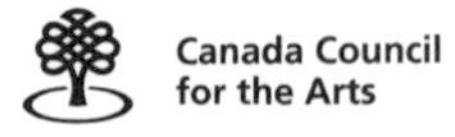

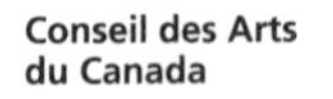

This book is dedicated to my family and each and every one of my past teammates.

Table of Contents

Foreword by Arron Asham (1)
Foreword by Jim Cuddy (5)
Introduction (7)
Quesnel, British Columbia 1991-93 (15)
Major Junior/NHL Draft 1993-97 (35)
Montreal/Freddy Beach 1995-99 (75)
From Long Beach to Utah to St. John's 1999-2000 (129)
Colorado Gold Kings and Hershey Bears 2000-01 (137)
Idaho Steelheads 2001-02 (159)
Cincinnati/Orlando 2002-03 (171)
The Last Decade (183)
The Conception Bay Comeback (203)
Why I Love the Game (219)

Foreword

by

Arron Asham

When Newf asked me to write a piece for his book, I wasn't sure where to start. (I call TR "Newf," by the way—that's what we all called him back in our Western Hockey League days.) I haven't done one of these things before, but Newf and I shared some great experiences and he's a good pal—so here we are. We were roommates on team road trips playing junior hockey for Red Deer, and when we made the transition from junior to pro we remained close as members of the Fredericton Canadiens and eventually the Montreal Canadiens. We spent a lot of time with the Habs as "black aces"—players who practised with the team as fifth-liners and wouldn't get into the lineup unless there was an injury to one of the veteran players. They were great times because the Habs were bringing us along slowly and giving us some experience with the big club. We had no pressure on us and could still claim we played for the Habs, so let's just say we had a lot of fun with that kind of status. Nearly every day, whether we were shopping for clothes, eating a meal, or having a beer, Newf would make eye contact with me and whisper, "Ash . . . can you fucking believe we play in the NHL?" I'm not exaggerating, either. On the road, when we hit some random pub, within a half an hour Newf would be on the mic, singing songs with the band while trying his hand at stand-up comedy between sets and talking about his hockey stories to anyone who would listen. He loved life and meeting new people. Newf's energy lit up the room, and I must admit I needed his incredibly honest, unique brand of humour sometimes. Pro hockey isn't as easy as you think. Sure, it comes with fame and glory, especially at the NHL level, but there's always pressure to perform, and you are only ever as good as your last shift. Even now, after more than a decade in the NHL, I can honestly tell you I never felt my job was safe. Probably because it never was. I learned what it took to be a good teammate from my buddy Newf, and it paid off. I am not taking anything away from my own accomplishment at all, I just think you need to pick things up along the way from your close friends, and Newf is a guy I shared a passion for hockey with and also an appreciation for our place in the game. I am not sure if we taught each other anything new, but we share similar characteristics on and off the ice and we'd usually bring out the best in each other. From the minute he came sauntering into our Red Deer Rebels dressing room in 1997 in his snakeskin cowboy boots, rambling on about his crazy experiences, I knew we'd get along.

During the 1998–99 season, we both played on the same line for Fredericton of the American Hockey League. Myself, Newf, and Scott King had pretty good seasons that year, and Newf and I got into more than our fair share of fisticuffs. We played in a tough division and were always ready to tangle because it usually meant giving the team a spark and showing the big club we were determined. Sometimes we were just pissed off, though; we both play with a bit of a temper!

We were in Hershey on one particular evening, playing in their old barn, the Hersheypark Arena, which had been around since the 1930s. I got into a few fights on the trip, and in one of them I had injured my right hand hitting a helmet. My hand was fractured but I could still shoot and pass. Getting into another fight would have been stupid, but once the game started I had words with Jeff Buchanan — a big, tough defender who was hard to play against. A few shifts into the second period, I told Newf I was gonna ask him to go. "Fuck that, Ash, we are playing well, man. Don't hurt your hand. One more period and this road trip is over, and we can currently call it a success," Newf said. "Moose (Dave Morissette, our toughest player) will go talk to him and settle things down. If you get into a tilt, you could be done for the year."

I agreed with Newf, but when we took the ice for the next shift, I still wanted a piece of Buchanan. We chirped a little more, but then out of nowhere Newf came storming in to save the day. The thing is, Jeff Buchanan was not only a big dude but he was a lefty — and neither of us realized that. Newf went into the fight blind figuratively and came out blind literally. The two combatants wailed away on each other, with Newf taking some real haymakers, nearly swelling both of his eyes shut at once. He also ended up fracturing his own hand in the fight. In the dressing room after the game, as blood still seeped out of one of the wounds around Newf's right eye, he looked up and asked me, "Did I go down, Ash, or did I stay up the whole fight?" I assured my buddy he stayed on his feet and as Newf undid his skates, half groggy, I saw him grin with pleasure. Ironically, I got called up a few days later, while Newf missed some time due to his broken hand.

That one story says a lot: Newf was a great teammate and sometimes people forget how good a player he was. He could score and fight with the best of 'em, and was one of the most underrated passers I've ever seen. Unfortunately, players who go hard tend to get hurt frequently, and after a while his body just couldn't take the rigours of playing 100 games a year. Hell, I'm surprised mine has held up this well.

Now Newf has written his book (I always encouraged him to do it but never thought it would actually happen). I promised him if this day ever came, I'd be there for him—just like he has been there for me, so many times, over the years. I am not sure what lies ahead in this book, but I can guarantee it'll be honest and interesting. Whenever I run into another ex-teammate of Newf's, the first thing we do is start trading "TR" stories, and I haven't heard a bad one yet. Finally, the hockey world is about to see what all the fuss is about.

Congrats, Newf, and thanks for always being a good pal.

Foreword

by

Jim Cuddy

To those of us who love the game of hockey, the lives of NHLers are unfathomably fascinating. We want to know everything: the way they were as kids, how early they knew they had a chance to play in the NHL, when they made it up to the Show . . . everything. We soak up all the details and compare them to the normal lives we know. This is the way we treat our heroes in Canada, and believe me, anyone who has played in the NHL, even for a single game, is a hero to us.

However, the true stories are rarely told. What we end up knowing is a small portion of the whole tale—the Coles Notes version, if you will. We get the highlights but none of the substance. What is excised is the real-life part: how they handled being told they were special, how they dealt with their first abusive coach, how they took their first demotion. If life is in the details, these are the details worth knowing.

Terry Ryan was a true prospect. He was drafted eighth overall by the historic Montreal Canadiens, and for a member of the great nation of Newfoundland, there could not be a better place to play hockey (well, maybe the Bruins, but that is another story). Terry was fast and talented, could score and fight, and the way ahead appeared bright indeed. He looked like a sure thing, so what could go wrong?

Well, we all know the path ahead can be thorny, and it certainly was for young Terry. Throw in a series of injuries, some ill-timed antics, Michel Therrien, and numerous other humorous setbacks, and you are no longer on track to be the next Gretzky. What starts out as "boy realizes his dream of playing in the NHL" soon becomes a morality play.

But the real story is one of a man with steely character, who plays hard and dangerously for his teammates. A young man who tells his story with honesty, humility, and a keen sense of humour no matter how ill-timed. We get the whole story here: no blemish removed, no Photoshopped memory, all in. It is a life laid bare, and we are left to draw our own conclusions about the career of one young Terry Ryan.

It is a rollicking story and, true to his word, Terry never holds back. He is, as are many of his Newfoundland brethren, a master storyteller. The reader is swept along by the vivid detail and remarkable memories. We are grateful for the honesty.

It is not easy to lead a public life and feel you have failed in the eyes of others. However, I believe the reverse is true. Terry Ryan has lived a life of fascinating possibilities, and he comes out a man of integrity and wisdom.

We should all be so lucky.

Introduction

I have two separated shoulders, an ankle that's been damaged beyond repair, and unstable knees. Irritating the elbows they were once attached to, numerous bone chips float inside me. The outside part of my right hand has been numb since 2001, when a skate lacerated my forearm's tendons. On cold days most of my joints hurt — especially my knuckles, and even more specifically the ones on my right hand. To date I've absorbed over 150 stitches, and my nose is crooked from being broken a half dozen times. Sometimes it hurts to breathe, and I am pretty certain it is due to the fact I once broke my ribs — collapsing a lung — and played through it. Scars line my body and pain lives under them.

I am a former professional hockey player, an eighth overall pick in the NHL Entry Draft. I am also the answer to this "Useless Sports Trivia" classic: What Montreal Canadiens first-rounder went three picks ahead of Jarome Iginla in 1995?

My name is Terry Ryan, Junior. And I am what would be considered in hockey circles — hell, in any sports circle — a first-round "flop."

I currently play senior hockey for three figures a week.

Why, you ask? For the same reason I wrote this book. I love the game: the team concept, the finesse, the toughness, the camaraderie . . . the whole experience. The game is beautiful. Most of life's important lessons can be taught not only on the ice but in the values that make a player a good teammate off of it. Learning to win is about learning to lead and succeed through unity. It requires acts of unselfishness that make you not only a better player but a better person. Hockey imitates life because the attributes it takes to be successful on the ice mirror the realities of the everyday grind. Life is full of ups and downs — and so is a hockey career. Learning to deal with it can be difficult and rewarding.

I want to point out that this isn't a traditional autobiography. These are simply stories that I have written down over the years. I edited them and connected the dots, and here we are. The game of hockey is simply the vehicle that made these stories possible. They are for the most part in chronological order, and some walk the fine line between hilarious and inappropriate, but I am not going to apologize. I have no regrets about any of them.

I was born in St. John's, Newfoundland, on January 14, 1977. My hometown is Mount Pearl. My father and mother are both from the Rock; my father played professional hockey (most notably for the World Hockey Association's Minnesota Fighting Saints) after a very successful junior career with the Hamilton Red Wings of the Ontario Hockey Association and retired from the game at the age of 26 — young for a prospect — using hockey as a catapult to a free degree and career as a French teacher. He taught me at a young age that the point of being a hockey player isn't all about making the NHL. He grew up one of five children; his mother raised the kids, and his father worked as a waiter at the Mount Peyton Hotel in Grand Falls. Dad had to work hard for everything he accomplished, and he set an example for me. My mother worked odd jobs her whole life, travelling wherever and whenever my father's career dictated. Eventually she did the same for me, knowing I needed my parents around for the first couple of years after I moved away to the mainland (my mother is a saint). My parents moved with me to Quesnel, British Columbia, when I was 14, giving up their jobs in the process, so that I could play in the Western Hockey League. They figured it was the appropriate league for me, and they were correct.

We moved to Quesnel in 1991, and at 14 I made the Quesnel Millionaires, a Junior A hockey club in northern BC, and that made me the youngest junior player in Canada at the time. I was 6 feet and 180, so I fit in on a size level, but most of these guys were 18 to 21, so needless to say I saw a lot that year and had to mature in a hurry, on and off the ice. It wasn't easy. Mount Pearl seemed light years away.

In 1992 I was drafted third overall in the WHL Bantam Draft by the Tri-City Americans. We had a good young team, and I still consider it a privilege to have played hockey with guys like Daymond Langkow, Brian Boucher, and Sheldon Souray. Those years are crucial in any young person's development, let alone a hockey player's. I lived up to my hype at that point and was selected 8th overall in the 1995 NHL Entry Draft. Lanks went 5th (Tampa Bay) and Bouch went 21st (Philly). It was a great experience and unique in the hockey world; not many junior teams have three guys taken in the first round of the NHL draft. Other than a brief stop in Red Deer in 1997 (a trade deadline deal sent me to the Red Deer Rebels), I was on to bigger and better (so-called) things.

I eventually turned pro, and outside of the odd NHL game, I played for the Canadiens farm team in Fredericton from 1997 to 1999 and put up good numbers. I could score and fight with the best in the league and figured NHL glory was in my immediate future.

But things don't always work out as envisioned. After being told in summer 1999 that I was not a serious candidate for the Montreal squad, I held out from camp. I didn't do it for more money; I wanted a better shot at playing in the Show than I felt I was getting. This turned out to be one of the most ridiculous decisions I've ever made, and looking back I don't know what I was thinking. My agent, Mike Barnett, was pretty confident I would be traded; he represented Wayne Gretzky, amongst others, so I figured he'd know. But I am certainly not blaming him for anything that went wrong in my career — I was the one who phoned and told him I wanted out. Besides, this kind of thing normally ended in a trade. Well, I didn't get one, and most of the other guys who were pegged for an NHL future did. Craig Conroy, Darcy Tucker, Tomas Vokoun, Brad Brown, Gordie Dwyer, Valeri Bure, Arron Asham . . . the list goes on.

In 2001, when I was released by Les Habitants, I had been long out of the hockey mainstream and had suffered a couple of significant injuries. I accepted a free agent tryout with the Dallas Stars, and one thing led to another and I hurt my ankle pretty bad. It was dubbed a high ankle sprain, and it never healed. Within two years my hockey career was over, and I was dumbfounded. Many athletes aren't prepared for life after sport, especially when the end comes prematurely.

Setbacks always present unintended circumstances, and many of them are positive ones. In 2003 I started a youth development program for disadvantaged youth in Newfoundland (in this case 12 Innu kids from northern Labrador) with good friends and ex-teammates Steve "Spock" Kelly, Todd Gillingham, and Matt Kolle. We called it "education through motivation": go to school, get an opportunity to play hockey — simple as that. We moved the kids from Labrador to Bell Island (a 20-minute ferry ride from St. John's) and stayed with them in a big house so they could be well prepared for their new lives. At the time, nobody from their community, Natuashish, had graduated from high school in over a decade. Drugs and alcohol were a problem, and they needed some direction. They needed so much direction that it made me wake up to the realities for some people who weren't as fortunate as I had been. It made my hockey worries seem ridiculous. I don't think I could be more proud when I tell you that three of them ended up graduating from high school and going to college — and we learned as much from them as they learned from us. I still keep in touch with some of the boys. Indirectly, hockey created these opportunities, and the boys were even mentioned that year on *Hockey Night in Canada*'s "Coach's Corner," with Ron MacLean and Don Cherry.

In 2008, while at a restaurant in Red Deer, Alberta, I ran into my wife-to-be, Danielle Koss Young Ryan, and my future stepson, Tison. Tison's biological father, B.J. Young, was one of my best buddies when we were rookies in Tri-Cities, and we finished our junior careers together playing on a line for the Red Deer Rebels in 1997. Danielle and BJ were an item back then, and we were all tight, learning to become adults together. BJ was killed in an automobile accident in 2005, and sometimes it makes me think that some things are meant to happen. Not BJ's tragedy, obviously, but randomly running into Danielle and Ty afterwards and now being a family: I didn't even know they were in Red Deer when I ran into them, and I had only been in Alberta briefly at the time. We have since added baby girl Penny-Laine, and although we live in Newfoundland, we keep close ties with Danielle's wonderful family in Penhold, Alberta, and visit a couple of times a year. Danielle's parents, Bruce and Lorraine Koss, are great people, and we've been friends since 1997, so in a way we've been a part of each other's lives for over 15 years. This made the transition from friend to family much easier. Her brother and sister, Shane and Trish, chat with us pretty much daily and visit frequently; the distance may be far but the bond is still tight.

Most people consider my hockey career a disappointment—and I can't really disagree with that. Still, I look at my life through very thankful, appreciative eyes. If I'd written a bucket list at the age of 12, it probably would have gone like this: 1) Travel to Europe, 2) See Disneyland, 3) Collect 200 CDs, 4) Play in the NHL—for the Montreal Canadiens.

Sometimes I still can't believe it's all happened—and I guess it's that feeling that motivates me to talk about it with pride and appreciation.

I still play hockey, as I mentioned. I live in Portugal Cove, Newfoundland, and every weekend I suit up in the Newfoundland Senior Hockey League for the Allan Cup–contending Clarenville Caribous. My ankle doesn't take as much wear and tear on a 24-game schedule, and because the pace is slower than it was in pro, I get by. But I am a shadow of the player I once was. Yes, I am older, and injuries have taken a toll. But you know what? I don't care one bit. I love the game and what it has done for me. Because of hockey I have formed lifelong friendships, travelled all over the world, met my idols, partied with celebrities, been on a reality show, attained a university degree, sung onstage with rock stars, and created opportunities for people less fortunate than myself. I also get to play for my country, on Canada's national ball hockey team, in the summers. I was raised by good people and have great friends, hundreds that I regularly keep in touch with.

As you read, you will probably note that I describe many things in great detail, and that I include lots of names/nicknames of friends I have made along the way. Many of these people you have never even heard of—but I feel it's important for them to be included because, essentially, this story isn't about me as much as my experiences (there is a huge difference). I don't care if people remember my statistics, but I do care that something resonates with them as a consequence of reading this book. The stories I have to tell are about a personal journey in the game of hockey. They are about finding my identity, which is forever changing and influenced by all the people I mention in the pages that follow. They've all stuck with me over the years. I'm glad I kept a journal, because I've taken something important from all these experiences.

Quesnel, British Columbia
1991–93

Welcome to the Wild West

Quesnel is a small mill town smack dab in the middle of British Columbia — everything above the Okanagan is considered northern BC. I had been brought out west by the Tri-City Americans, who wanted to make me their first-round selection that year. I had to actually move to western Canada in order to be eligible for the WHL draft, as I had played all my minor hockey in Mount Pearl, Newfoundland.

I was really nervous. My father, as I said, had played pro hockey, and I put all my trust in him because this was a big move and I was too young to really know much about it. On the plane I remember him saying that it was up to me, I could bail on this idea at any time and he would support me. Still, he said that he had seen and played a lot of hockey, and in his opinion I was a bona fide NHL prospect (being 6 feet tall and 180 pounds at 14 didn't hurt). Another point he made was that I had to do my best to fit in once we got to Quesnel. These guys were older, so I had to be ready to grow up and mature a little faster than the kids I had been hanging with to this point, who were back in Newfoundland, starting grade nine. This meant a lot of changes — on and off the ice. On the ice, the biggest challenge was the size and physicality. I had come from peewee the year before, where there was no hitting, let alone fighting. This was a league for big boys, Dad said, and it would be easier to get respect if I didn't show signs of weakness. Off the ice the differences were obvious between a kid my age and these dudes, so I had to be ready to mature quickly!

Now, I don't want to make it seem like I was a saint as an early teen, because I wasn't. A few of my buddies — Gary "the Shark" Clarke, Mike "Smitty" Smith, and Jeremy "Taz" Charles — and I were into mischief here and there. We'd often put Vaseline and pepper on our faces and pull a hat down over our heads in order to give the impression we were old enough to be in the bar, and go to strip clubs to see naked women; we would collect beer bottles "for our minor hockey team" and spend the money on porn mags and pellet guns; we'd buy eggs and throw them at our buddies' houses . . . things like that. We bent the rules and had fun, but I was a good student and a decent fella.

But now my maturation had to accelerate — and it wasn't easy for a while. The whole first year was eye-opening and unforgettable. Girls, booze, parties, sexual frustration, acne — I had to deal with all this on top of beginning high school in a foreign place!

The first few days were tough, and I remember it being very obvious that I was nervous and awkward, although my actual play on the ice was average in relation to the other guys — and for a 14-year-old that was more than you could ask for. Camp was going well and now it was time for the first exhibition game, which was only a big deal to one person in the building — me. The league — the Rocky Mountain Junior Hockey League — had a reputation as one of the toughest junior circuits in Canada. Quesnel is a blue-collar town; many fans came to see the fights and hits more than anything else. If the team won, it was a bonus. By the way, I don't consider this a bad thing. I still have a lot of friends there and visit frequently. Good people, good values. But don't piss anyone off, or it's go time. I learned a lot in that small town, and I think it helped shape my character.

It was game day, and it was time to eat our pre-game meal. For hockey players, a game day usually consists of a skate in the morning, pre-game meal at around noon, a nap, and off to the rink by 5 for a 7 p.m. game. This was the first time I'd perform that game day routine, and I remember it vividly.

Things were a little sketchy from the get-go. I remember trying to be funny, to gain acceptance from the older, more experienced guys. I was still getting to know them, though, and it was hard for me to differentiate the leaders, the selfish, the nerds, and so forth. To me, they were all to be looked up to because of nothing more than age.

You Wanna Go, Kid?

I remember my hands sweating, which hardly ever happens — I wanted to be accepted, plain and simple. I wanted to be able to relax and until I hung out a little and actually played a game, I knew that wouldn't happen. I met up with a few of the guys for brunch in the early afternoon, but my anxiousness was obvious. When the waiter came to take our orders, he announced the specials. At the end of his spiel, he said, "Oh yeah, and we have any breakfast, anytime." Trying to impress by using a little wit, I answered back: "In that case, I am gonna go with an Egg McMuffin and some Denny's pancakes during the Ice Age."

Everyone froze, and the waiter challenged me to a fight, believe it or not. Had I not been with my teammates, I was in for a beat-down for sure! Funny thing is, when I got to the rink and retold the story, they all laughed and thought it was a great comeback, but confessed to not understanding me at the time because of my Newfoundland accent, which made sense. I had a thick one back then. That was another obstacle I sometimes forget about while reminiscing. Even though we all spoke English, there was a little bit of a language barrier.

We were playing the Williams Lake Mustangs, and before the game the guys made me feel as comfortable as possible. Ron Coleman, our coach at the time, put me in the starting lineup. The building was full . . . it was my first game . . . everyone was staring at the flag during the singing of the national anthem . . . starting lineups were announced . . . the referee waved at both goalies . . . it was time for puck drop! Breathing in and finally managing a smile and sigh of relief that the waiting was finally over, I got set for the opening faceoff.

Well, I should have expected the unexpected, because apparently a Williams Lake player who shall remain nameless was ready to teach me a lesson. He cross-checked me in the face without hesitation and dropped his gloves before I could say "Nintendo," and I went down. I was caught off guard, and when I got up, everyone was goin' at it. Our defencemen were skating at the Williams Lake bench. My linemates Chris Spencer and Dave Standing—two great lads who would later deal with anyone who dared look at me the wrong way—were goin' toe to toe, old-school style, and as I looked up from my "turtle" position I saw the goalies actually pass Spence and Davey. Now *they* were going at it. Coaches were yelling and even some fans were mixin' it up. It happened fast, but it seemed like it was taking place in slow motion, and I remember deciding to just roll with it.

I got up and went at my dancing partner with reckless abandon and pent-up rage. The ice looked like a yard sale as I dodged a couple of helmets and regained my footing. I grabbed my opponent's jersey, pulled back to deliver a punch to his big, fat melon, and . . . I got my head punched in. Although I don't remember feeling the blows (with so much adrenaline flowing they rarely hurt at the time), I remember the linesmen coming to my rescue. I couldn't really see much of the melee going on around me with blood flowing down my head in front of my eyes and the officials escorting me to our dressing room.

I was whisked behind the door along with the rest of the starting lineup, one by one, and as it closed behind us I started to process all of the preceding events. I will never forget the moment—it plays like a home video in my cerebrum. Spence walked over and hugged me and told me not to worry. He said they were always going to be close by for the next two years, and nobody would mess with me in or away from the hockey rink. My dad came into the room. Davey opened a beer and passed it to me (we had been ejected from the game), and that was the first sip of beer I had in front of one of my parents. I know that sounds awful to many parents out there, but it was symbolic. Giving me the beer wasn't to get me drunk, it was to welcome me to junior hockey. People have to adapt to different circumstances when growing up, I guess, and my childhood life in Newfoundland—at least during the winters—was but a memory. I was closer to a man than a boy that day.

I started to laugh—and cry. I think most of it was tears of joy as all that built-up tension was released. Now I really felt like a Quesnel Millionaire. I felt as if I finally had something in common with the many Canadian icons I had looked up to since I first tuned in to *Hockey Night in Canada*.

So there it is: a fight before a bodycheck, and a beer before a goal. And friends for life.

Retribution

I didn't forget what happened that first game. Days passed and the exhibition season finally came to a close. I think we played five or six times, but I can't be sure, and I can't tell you what our win-loss record was—all I remember was that I felt more comfortable each and every game. It takes a while to get used to the speed and timing of a league as you move up the ladder, and I had skipped eight levels, so I was shaky at first. I got hit with my head down, a lot.

The time was coming to play Williams Lake again, and I was quite understandably nervous because I'd be addressing the meatball who kicked the shit out of me the first game. I had to have my payback, and this time it wasn't for the boys, it was for me. I had too much pride for this donkey to be taking out his anger on me and using my face for a punching bag/stress reliever.

I called my linemates and we met for coffee. I was hunting for the best advice I could get on how to prove my point. Dave Standing, Chris Spencer, and I were joined by our captain, Ashley Fennell. Ash was a good guy who loved the game. An Edmonton kid, born and raised, he would routinely show up at Quesnel Secondary School to make sure us high school guys were doing alright and not skipping class. Dave Standing was a former super-prospect who got a little sidetracked in his teen years and never pursued hockey or took it as seriously as he should have until he was 19 and it was a little too late. Davey was a loyal guy, and it became evident that he didn't want me making the same mistakes as he did. Chris Spencer? Well, Spence is one of the toughest men I have ever seen, pound for pound. He was almost 6 foot but real slender at 175 pounds and frequently fought players much bigger. Spence had a high threshold for pain. He was brought up in northern BC, in a place called Mackenzie, and he was one of those dudes who commanded respect upon first glance. I will never forget, as long as I live, the time he got hit and punctured a lung during a very rough first period in Fort St. John. Spitting up blood, he not only finished the game but tried to hide it from the rest of the team because he didn't want any attention brought to himself.

After an hour or so of shooting the shit, the plan was simple. Dump the puck in this gronk's corner and let Spence have at him. Fairly easy, right? Well fuck that. I had other plans.

During warm-up we were treated to a blaring medley of hard rock songs as the place filled up. Spence stared into the Mustangs zone. He didn't say anything, and in this case his actions spoke way louder than his words. I could tell the whole Williams Lake team knew it was going to be a rough one. They hadn't forgotten what happened last time either.

As is usually the case in games with a lot of tension and expectation for a stepped-up level of physical play, things started out a little slow. Nobody wanted to make the first move. I felt the tension in the air, looked at the fans, looked at the Mustangs bench, and looked at my teammates. I would have to say the moment right before hockey retribution is one of the biggest rushes in sports. Most hockey fights aren't premeditated, though. In fact, later in my career I would have handled the situation differently, but let's face it, I was still a super-rookie with a temper who had a lot to learn.

The first period was winding down when I skated to the Williams Lake bench with a few rehearsed one-liners. "Hey Meatball," I said. "I bet you would be the toughest guy in my math class. I mean, sure, you're six years older, but the word on the street is you like beating up kids, and you're pretty good at it. Plus, you have reason to be upset. My bruises from last game healed, but your face will always look like that! Tough break, asshole."

Their captain, Lenny Forschner, actually started laughing. Even I was astonished I had gone ahead with phase one of my ridiculous plan. I had Meatball's attention, and people on the benches and in the crowd stared in disbelief and anticipation. Meatball jumped over the boards and skated towards me, ever so slowly, licking his banged-up lips like a predator closing in on his prey.

We met at centre ice, and once again he knocked me down with the first punch. But I got up and grabbed on and actually began fighting back. I could feel my nose blood trickling down the back of my throat.

What happened next I don't think anyone could have predicted.

I was wrestling with this guy, trying to get close, and got a few rabbit punches in. I was basically caught in a wrestling match, which is exactly what I wanted. My hands were all over him, groping his face, head, and jersey while he peppered the back of my head. He kept throwing punches but never got any big ones in — I was doing okay and hanging in there. His hands were a bloody mess, and he was hitting my helmet more than anything. After I could sense him getting tired, I started coming back with a couple of haymakers of my own. The crowd was into it, my team was cheering me on, and his team was in shock. Finally the fight came to an end as I threw down my opponent and raised my hands in victory, proudly staring into the crowd. I must say, for a brief moment I felt like a Roman gladiator. As I skated towards the dressing room, I knew I had made an impact on my status in school as well. Things were good.

After the game, the boys all high-fived me and admitted they hadn't seen that coming. They asked, "Newf, how the hell did you pull that off?"

"Well, boys," I said with a grin and a nod, "I appreciate that you all look out for me, but this was personal. I knew he was gonna try something, so I figured I would beat him to the punch. I shaved the sides of my helmet down with a file (I learned that from a local legend in Quesnel—a tough guy named Jason Helzel), and when he was hitting me it was actually ripping the skin from his hand." Now everyone was staring at me with open ears and open mouths. "Then I put hot sauce all over my hands so that when we got in tight I would rub it in his eyes so he was unable to focus clearly for the rest of the fight. After that, I just plain kicked the shit outta him."

The boys were flabbergasted, to say the least. But I can tell you with a straight face that although I got in many other skirmishes that year, I wasn't ever considered a pushover again, and people thought twice before attempting an encounter with me! At season's end, I was the leading scorer of a Junior A franchise and focused on the NHL draft in a few years time.

Necessary Roughness

I know that story's a little violent. But that's the way hockey can be. At 14, of course, that doesn't usually happen, and it shouldn't. Fourteen-year-olds play minor hockey and my jump to junior at that age was extremely rare, but there is truth in the fact that once kids get to junior hockey they have to learn how to fend for themselves and be good teammates. Not everyone has to fight; as people start to understand themselves as players, they get comfortable with their boundaries on the ice, and by the time you are a professional, the hockey world has a pretty good idea of what kind of player you are. I admit, I got into a few fights just because there were scouts in the stands evaluating me and if I had a bad game, I figured I could always show them some spunk by grabbing a monster and challenging him to a tilt. I usually did it for a reason, and those reasons were justifiable within the context of the game but not always necessary. If a guy hit our goalie, for example, it was go time. If the team needed a boost and we were being out-hit by the opponent, I'd find a willing combatant, ideally one who was bigger than me, so a win became a huge lift for our squad. If our best player got hit by a cheap shot? I'd track down the culprit and start throwin' haymakers! You have to think like a warrior.

I am in no way comparing sports to being in the military, but I always looked up to my grandfather, Bill Norris, who passed away when I was 13 years old. I was very close to him; Pop came to every practice or game I ever played in any sport and was so proud of me it makes me shiver and brings a tear to my eye as I write this. He loved me so much. He would tell me stories about the war and how you have to think like a team in order to get through every day. Check your ego at the door, try to park your emotions and focus. He lost his right arm in World War II while fighting aboard the famous HMS *Bulldog*—a British Navy destroyer that changed the direction of the war by capturing coding documents from a German submarine. Pop would talk about his deceased pals like they were still alive, his eyes lighting up at the very mention of their names. He was one of the founders of the Mount Pearl branch of the Royal Canadian Legion; he and his chums seemed like they not only enjoyed each other's company—they needed it. They hung out daily and played cards while I sat around absorbing their stories and admiring their maturity. I can't relate to some of the things they must have experienced, but one thing I do know is that being around those gentlemen helped me gain an edge in team sports. I am subpar at individual sports like tennis and golf, but I play above expectations in hockey, ball hockey, and baseball because of the influence of the war vets. Team success is based on sacrifice. Good players become great when they are humble. You have to buy into a system and do whatever it takes to win; you can't just use your individual skill set to get shit done. Your team becomes your family. Just like Pop and his pals, I now sit around and tell stories with retired players, some of whom I didn't even know when I played. We need that connection as well.

I dropped the mitts a little too often for some people's liking—and maybe that opinion is totally justified—but there is no denying I went higher in the draft because I had 207 PIMs to go along with the 50 snipes. My good pal Zach O'Brien from St. John's led the Quebec Major Junior Hockey League in 2011–12 with 50 goals as well, but had zero PIMs (yes, zero, as in none the entire season) to go along with those statistics, and I guarantee you that played a part in him being undrafted. The thing is, you can't teach the level of talent that Z-Man possesses, but you can definitely teach a guy to be a little grittier, and I have no doubt Zach will be a fantastic pro someday—hopefully in the NHL—once he learns to play with a little more edge. We've trained together for a couple of summers now, and when I watched Zach play in 2012–13 the improvement in his all-around game was very noticeable. He had close to the same statistics but played with more grit, and therefore many teams are calling him now, offering tryouts. You learn as you go. Family friend Teddy Purcell is one of Tampa Bay's best players and he went through the same thing. Ryane Clowe of the New Jersey Devils left home a dangler and makes his living as a grinder. You don't have to overdo it like I did, but getting by from shift to shift in pro hockey requires a bit more nutsack than it does in junior and way more than it does in college, and the sooner you realize that the better. There is no denying a small-statured guy like Darcy Tucker had NHL success because of his willingness to put his body on the line for his team. There is also no denying Sid Crosby is a better athlete because he's an ultra-skilled player who thinks team first. We have all seen skilled players who don't play with that kind of mindset—Alexei Yashin, anyone?—fizzle and underachieve, leaving their fans and teammates mystified. On a scale of 1 to 10, if a guy's skill is a 10 but his give-a-fuck meter is a 2, I would avoid him at all costs. It never works unless the player has an attitude overhaul. Fans and players know it—they can see it happening—yet teams do it again and again, hoping their new signing had an attitude overhaul in the off-season.

And it brings the team down too. When an asshole is signed to a squad—usually for top dollar—the other players become demoralized. Knowing they have to work with the jerk makes life worse no matter how you cut it. I play a pretty clean game and usually don't take many penalties outside of fights, but whenever I get a chance to play against a fucking asshole ex-teammate, I give him a root with my stick just to let him know I'm game whenever he wants to dance.

Toughness comes in many forms. I've always said, if you're a bad fighter or don't wanna fight, don't! I don't think it's for everyone, and fighting is just one small element of toughness. Peter Forsberg, for example, was always one of the toughest players on the ice because he was tenacious and always wanted the biscuit. He'd go into the corner with Chuck Norris and a blindfold if it meant having a better chance to win the game, and he'd leave said corner using a toothpick and whistling a tune. He won every battle out there and his career—though long and brilliant—was cut a little short because the heart he wore on his sleeve and tenacity he brought to the table every night resulted in a slew of nagging injuries. Every interview Peter ever gave always saw him emphasize the concept of team importance, and when his team lost you could see it tear his heart out. Mr. Forsberg single-handedly changed my opinion of European players, and now that I have many Euros as good pals, I thank him for it. He wasn't even on my team, but I learned as much from him by studying his actions as I did from Shayne Corson in Montreal, one of the toughest men you'll ever come across, on or off the ice. Cors didn't take any shit out there.

Before I move on to another Quesnel tale, I want to finish this little rant about being a team player and toughness with a story about one of my best buddies in the game, Mike Hurley. After Quesnel, Mike and his brother Mark, who is two years older, played on my junior team in the WHL for three years. They have a great sense of humour and we lived close to each other in Pasco, Washington, which along with Kennewick and Richland make up the Tri-Cities. The hockey life for us at the time was filled with new experiences every day. Coming from playing minor hockey games in Sherwood Park (their hometown) with a handful of fans, to playing in front of sellout crowds in Portland or Seattle, is overwhelming, intense, and exhilarating. This is the case for almost all kids who share that experience, and that's why these dudes remain your close pals in life; you can identify with them. I sympathize with athletes who are not involved in team sports and have to move away from home; having to go through all that life-adjustment by yourself must be lonely.

Mike Hurley is 6-foot-1, about three inches taller than Mark and slightly skinnier. With his baby face, he could pass for someone five years younger, so in junior hockey this physical appearance combined with his natural finesse play made him look like a child playing amongst men. At first glance, this non-physical, boyish-looking right winger for Tri-Cities would cause a double take, and the thought of him ever becoming an offensive presence in the WHL seemed crazy, even to me, when he first arrived in 1994.

The more I got to know Mike, however, the more faith I had in him. Mike was punctual and determined and did what it took to succeed in all aspects of life. He took university courses in junior and posted great marks. He showed up half an hour early for every practice. He worked out in the gym tirelessly, and by the end of his second year with us he had added 25 pounds to his small frame. Mike wasn't what you'd call a tough player per se, but he did his job out there and finished his checks. In his first year of junior he had two goals, four assists, and six penalty minutes (of course, some of this is due to ice time, but he had to learn the ropes). Mike's focus on and off the ice catapulted him to 32 goals in his second year with our squad, and he chipped in with 34 penalty minutes. Five of those PIMs were for a fight after one of Spokane's players ran our goalie and we were losing. Mike saw our goalie down, dropped his gloves and got pumped, but he gave the boys a huge boost by showing he'd stick up for us. We came back and won the game. In Mike's final year of junior hockey—1997–98—he exploded for 50 goals (he also had 79 PIMs) and was dealt at the trade deadline deal to the Portland Winterhawks, who were hosting the Memorial Cup, the Holy Grail of junior hockey. The Winterhawks were a deep team and along with the likes of Brenden Morrow, Marian Hossa, and Andrew Ference (and others, including Todd Robinson, a small kid with rare offensive talent who deserved a better shot at the Big Show), Mike got the job done and sent the city of Portland into a frenzy. Simultaneously, I was sent onto the floor of my Fredericton apartment as I jumped off the couch with joy seeing him skate around the ice on television, hoisting hockey's hardest trophy to win.

In the summer of 2011, Mike had an accident. At a golf tournament in Kelowna, BC, he was left paralyzed after a fluke golf cart mishap. I had spoken to him that morning on the phone, so my memory of Mike on his worst day is one of love and friendship—which isn't really relevant, but it's something I still find curious. I gave the family space, and other than reading the odd update from Mark on mass email, I left the situation alone. I cried at night, reminded of the horrors of other teammates who suffered worse fates and are now six feet under. I would struggle with accepting his fate, and when I found out his wife was a month pregnant at the time of his accident, I was devastated for him. His family is fantastic. It's hard to be squeaky clean and cool at the same time, but they are just that. Good people with great morals.

In June 2012 I was attending my sister-in-law Trish Bauer's wedding in Red Deer, and as I always do when I am in town, I called up the boys — a bunch of the old junior crew who live in the area. We decided to meet at a restaurant in Edmonton not far from Whyte Avenue, and Mike was the last to arrive. I hadn't seen him since his life-changing event, and I hoped nobody would notice that I was shaking nervously. I didn't know how to handle the situation. I had seen worse things happen to strangers, but not to close chums. This was the first time I would ever see a once-super-athletic specimen like Mike have to wheel himself around. I felt pity and was uncomfortable. Then, outta nowhere, Mike rolled around the corner with a smile from ear to ear and high-fived me. "Neeeewwwfff!" he said, as if nothing happened. "So good to see you!"

Mike told me right off the bat about what happened that horrific day (in order to get the elephant out of the room, he said) and then he showed me pictures of the most recent addition to his family, a baby boy named Kane. He still played what sports he could and had adjusted quite well to life from a new perspective, happy to be alive and healthy. He looked as fit as ever and as we sipped on beer and talked about the glory days, I just couldn't help but laugh at the irony of the situation. In junior, Mike would look up to my toughness and brag about the fact that his buddy Newf had no fear and would take on any challengers. He came to see me get drafted and had his own modest professional career in the East Coast Hockey League, always keeping in touch as we exchanged stories about new cities and new experiences. Mike loved the fact that I fought Tie Domi, and brings it up to this day. But I want him to know something: Mike, you have taught me more about the power of human will than I could ever teach you, and you are tougher than I ever was, pal.

The 14-Year-Old Virgin

As the 1991–92 season reached the quarter mark, things were going better than expected. We were in last place in our division, but Quesnel had a history of being a cellar-dweller, and at least this year there were a few reasons to watch. We weren't getting blown out, and we were a tough bunch, which was a good enough good reason to go to most games.

Personally, I was feeling more comfortable on the ice with each shift, and at school I was finding my niche. My roommate, Mike Collins, who was the team captain the previous season (a genuine friend who passed away a few years ago) made my transition as smooth as possible and made sure I was on task. With hockey, that is. He'd come get me from class, and I'd skip school in the afternoon to work on my shot and things like that. When my mom confronted Mike about missing school, Mike would laugh and say I wasn't gonna score 50 goals from the science lab! He'd spar with me to make me tougher.

I am not going to lie, though, the whole high school environment was taking a while to get used to, and as a Newfoundlander it was sometimes tough to tell if they were laughing with me or at me. This, for the most part, I didn't give a shit about, but I didn't pass up any opportunities to fit in and do whatever it was the "cool" kids were doing.

In late November the team got some great news, and the news was music to my ears. We had another bantam-aged player coming in to play with us. This gave me a chance to hang with someone who was going through the exact same thing as me — or at least the closest thing to it. Fifteen-year-old defenceman Sheldon Souray was coming to town.

Sheldon has been an NHL all-star, so I have to assume 99 percent of the people reading this book are somewhat familiar with his good looks, cool demeanour, and hockey-playing ability, but all that was in its rawest form when this "city boy" from Edmonton came to town. Sheldon helped me immensely by seeing life through a very optimistic point of view, always. He was 15 years old, a few months older than me, with a very high level of confidence. When we got together at school or at a party, he made a point to talk to everyone. He usually ended up being the centre of attention without even realizing it. I tended to get intimidated, I think at first because everything was so new and I was so far away from home. Sheldon had come from the hockey hotbed of Edmonton, growing up watching what is arguably the best hockey team ever assembled in the NHL — the Oilers of the '80s. By contrast I had been to exactly three NHL games, two on a hockey trip to Quebec in peewee, and another under the same circumstances in Toronto. He was big, tough, and he had the attitude to make it, and we all knew it. The on-ice rough stuff I spoke of earlier didn't seem to faze Sheldon. Girls liked him. With Sheldon, you always had the feeling he had your back and everything would work out, no matter what.

So here we were, November sometime, and the hockey parties usually morphed into everybody-from-high-school parties. Let's face it, in a small town like that everyone ends up at the same place at the end of the night. In Q-Town it was what they called the "four-by." This was basically a huge fire burning in a field as teenagers' cars blared tunes on their new stereo systems with the bass turned up to competing levels of obnoxious noise. While out cruising, one of the cool cats of QSS could always be mistaken for a small earthquake or a herd of elephants in the distance. As the noise got closer, the sound usually turned out to be Metallica, AC/DC, Megadeth, or *Dance Mix '92*. There were often dust-ups. I remember this one evening as if it were yesterday — because it had a profound effect on the rest of my week . . . and year. Hell, it had an effect on the rest of my life!

Our team all headed up to the four-by after the game to have a few sodas. For Sheldon and me, that meant not getting caught out late by my parents. (My family kept a close eye on Sheldon, as his parents visited often but didn't live in BC.) All my buddies were there, but there were also some strangers — and one in particular caught my eye. It was the girl who sat next to me in history class and wore her jeans tighter than Dwight Yoakam after a week of all-you-can-eat buffets. You see, there was another curious change taking place — my interest in women.

She walked over, kindly gave me the rest of one of her Kokanees, and asked me to join her alone in a spot she had scoped out on the far side of the fire. I looked over at a blanket that was already set up. I froze and my body started shaking uncontrollably, but I played it as cool as I could.

Now, looking back, I can't imagine two people more unprepared for sex, or a less desirable setting. Metallica, beers, fights, fire — all of the above were prevalent as we tried to make passion happen. I remember thinking what a great story it would be. Even back then I was all about the story . . .

Well, the time had come (no pun intended). It was put up or shut up, and a few of the boys — if not all of them — knew what was going down but let me go with the flow without getting in the way. I had lied and said I had been laid a dozen times, but this was only to avoid a guaranteed onslaught of ribbing, and I am pretty sure the boys saw through that whole act. As we approached the intended destination, I proceeded to make numerous idiotic comments, including the always popular "the weather is pretty nice for November," in order to get her in the mood.

From the start, I thought it was an awful idea, and I figured right. We were awkward. We lay down without any kissing or foreplay and took off our pants. We decided to leave our tops on to keep warm, and my date lay down and assumed the sacred position. Being as cold as it was, even an ultra-horny virgin like myself had trouble getting it up, but after closing my eyes and daydreaming I felt my pants starting to tighten. I thought about one of my teachers back home—a sexy woman who shall remain unnamed but whose cleavage was sprinkled into most of my sexual thoughts. Now all I had to do was put on the condom, but my date beat me to the punch. She hauled one out of her pocket, continuing the movie-like romance we had going, and slipped it on me. This proved too much of a turn-on for me, and lo and behold I let loose in the condom before the act had even begun.

I couldn't let this happen. Nobody could know I just had an orgasm while the condom was being slipped on, or my reputation would be ruined just as it was gaining momentum. The whole situation was embarrassing enough; this premature happy ending would surely make matters worse, so I had to think fast, and that meant I had to keep on truckin'. I wedged myself between her legs and all of a sudden I was the king of the universe! We were cold, damp, and uncomfortable. I was working on round number two, but it didn't matter. I was so excited that it was actually happening. I was getting laid! I couldn't stop smiling, but at the same time I cannot see any possible way in which this poor girl got any enjoyment whatsoever out of the situation.

We were hot and heavy for what seemed like an hour but was probably four or five minutes. I was almost ready to finish again, when all the vehicles' lights came on in unison, pointing straight at us. I guess word had gotten out I was balls-deep, and most people in attendance were now onlookers to a ridiculous sexual spectacle. It was a display of the horizontal bop by two people who had no business taking part in the act. I was almost finished, and the chants began. In the distance you could hear my teammates: "Newf, Newf, Newf . . ."

Talk about pressure! At least 200 people were watching me sow my wild oats for the first time, and oddly enough they were chanting my name in full support of the decision I had made. I finally finished and stood up with my hands raised in victory and my pants down in guilt. I looked down at my lover, thanked her and ran back to the fire, not sure whether to be embarrassed or proud. It was surreal, to say the least, and most people in attendance were in disbelief. I should mention that on top of all this I had a haircut from hell, as the boys had carved a bad mohawk into my head during a heavy hazing session in Fernie while on the road. I distinctly remember the laughs afterwards. Even some teachers were there that night. Needless to say, Monday was awkward, especially history class.

Major Junior/NHL Draft
1993–97

The place they call the Tri-Cities in the WHL is made up of three small cities in south-central Washington State: Richland, Pasco, and Kennewick. Spokane is almost a two-hour drive northeast, Seattle three hours northwest, and Portland almost three hours southwest. The WHL's Tri-City Americans have called the area home since 1988. Despite some ups and downs, the team is still around after changing hands over the years. The owners now include two former players—Olaf Kolzig and Stu Barnes—who went on to great NHL careers. The franchise has been very successful in recent years, and although they have yet to win the Memorial Cup—given to junior hockey's best team every May—they have become a consistent contender for the league title, and that isn't easy to achieve in junior hockey, due to the heavy turnaround of players because of age limitations. (It is also difficult to predict how well an adolescent will adapt to junior.)

When I played for Team Newfoundland in the Vancouver Super Series as a peewee-aged bantam player and won the tournament's Most Promising Player award (I was in shock; I still wear the ring!), Ron Toigo, who now owns the WHL's Vancouver Giants franchise, was on hand with the Ams coach at the time—NHL legend Glenn "Chico" Resch—and promised me that if I moved to BC they'd draft me into the league with their first pick, and that's how I ended up in Quesnel in the first place. Ron told my father he would get him a job substitute-teaching in Quesnel and also pay him to be a scout. This situation worked out well for me, because the Americans ended up sending a few prospects to play with us at the Junior A level in hopes of grooming them into a prominent role with the big club. It wasn't unlike the way the NHL and AHL interact with each other, minus the big contracts. My father, it turns out, ended up doing his fair share for the club as well, helping myself and Sheldon Souray adjust to junior hockey in northern British Columbia. He also played a big part in getting my good pal Ryan Marsh (who was hell-bent on signing a deal with Northern Michigan University) to Tri-Cities.

Although Ryan never made it to the NHL, he is an example of the kind of success that doesn't produce NHL-level fame but is well worth the price of leaving home and meeting hockey's physical and mental demands for years on end. As captain of the University of Alberta Golden Bears, Ryan ended up winning multiple Canadian Interuniversity championships, and he also played a couple of years professionally for the Louisiana IceGators and Columbus Chill of the ECHL. He is a successful teacher in Edmonton and has a great family. Ryan and I ended up playing together for a season in Quesnel and three with the Ams. Those late teenage years are critical in a young man's development as a person, and we shared a lot of life-changing moments together.

To understand the Tri-Cities hockey experience, you need to realize the place is in the desert. I didn't think landscape like this existed so far north—but it does. Although close to all those bigger northwest cities I mentioned earlier, TC receives way less rain. Maybe this has something to do with the Rocky Mountains, which are not visible there but control the weather along their coastal path to the west. It gets cold at times, yes, but there is seldom snow (the threat of any snowfall at all may result in a day off school) and the spring and summer months are hotter than the real housewives of the NHL.

For the vast majority of my stay in TC, I lived with Drew "Shoey" Schoneck and Zenith "Zeke" Komarniski. We were billeted with Mark and Nancy Eby—fantastic people I don't call nearly enough anymore. It is easy to lose touch, but I think the work that the billets do is highly underappreciated. All former players should keep in touch with their billets if they had a good experience. I mean, those years from 16 to 20 are so very important as an athlete and as a person, if a kid is not handled correctly he may not fulfill his capabilities on or off the ice.

Shoey was 20 when I was 16, so we couldn't have been further apart in terms of age, but we got along great and killed time by fishing and playing roller hockey. Zeke was a year younger than me, and we had more battles as roommates. Once, early in our union, Zeke put hot sauce on my toothbrush. I didn't notice the red tinge on the bristles because my gums would bleed when I brushed them, and it sent me into a state of absolute panic, the hottest sensation I had ever experienced. Zeke started laughing from his bedroom and I snapped so loud I scared the shit out of Mark and Nancy, but all they could do was laugh. I don't blame them, I guess. After all, as Mark pointed out, I was supposed to be the team prankster, so I got what was coming to me.

I held my composure, went into the bathroom in the middle of the night, and got my revenge. I dumped out Zeke's cologne—"Cool Water," by Davidoff—and took a piss into the bottle. I figured this would be not only fun but ironic, as Zeke had a huge nose but couldn't smell for shit because it had been broken so many times. I told the boys and the kids at school not to say anything about his odour if they knew what was good for them, because you could smell Zenith coming a mile away. It worked, and good ol' Zeke wore my piss proudly to school for over a week before someone blew the whistle, and by that point I didn't give a shit!

The only other time I recall someone trying to prank me was when Jerry Frederickson, our trainer, put my skates into a freezer before practice. I then took a wizz in his apple juice and tricked him into guzzling it in front of the whole team! I was ruthless. I hated looking over my shoulder and enjoyed being in on all prank-related activity. Jerry knew better than to screw with me, and he paid the price for it.

As long as we are talking about Zenith's nose, I'll mention the fact that it was the subject of one of my favourite digs. A fan of the Tacoma Rockets (now Kelowna) used to have this big tube-like contraption he would yell into — like a loudspeaker, but homemade. He'd scream into one end and bend the other over the glass (he sat in the first row, by the blueline). One day while Zeke skated through the neutral zone, the guy yelled: "Hey Ref, Komarniski is offside, his nose is in by the net." I laughed and he continued, "And Ryan, what the fuck are you laughin' at! You're a dipshit with stupid fuckin' hair. But at least you can cut your hair. Komarniski can't escape that nose." Zeke was laughing too. That guy had some great chirps. I hope he reads this passage, wherever he is. They lost their team eventually, and he must have been heartbroken.

Brent Ascroft was a real good pal. He, Geoff Lynch, and I actually stayed in Kennewick to graduate from high school at the end of the 1993–94 hockey season (most guys transferred back home). Brent was an American from Rochester, New York, and a big-time blue chip prospect as a 16-year-old. They called him "Double-Nickel" because he wore number 55. Brent never played a game in the NHL — or even minor pro — but is an example of an under-the-radar success story I like to remind hockey parents about; he played five years in the WHL and used all the school scholarship money he was allotted in that time to earn a degree from Ohio State University after his junior career was done. Double-Nickel felt he was too small to play professionally even though his junior stats were superb. He played hard for a small-statured guy too, and is one of the all-time leaders in the WHL in games played, with 355; he missed only two games in his career, and those were when half our team got food poisoning on a trip to Moose Jaw (Brent and I were roommates and were so sick we vomited side by side into buckets for half a day and our tongues turned black from dehydration. The story actually got published in the *Hockey News*). He opted to guarantee himself a degree from a reputable university, and when he walked out of the dressing room for the last time after his fifth and final season, he tossed his skates in the garbage and hasn't put them on since! It's an odd thing to do, but I have to say I respect the man for it. He used hockey to his advantage and got exactly what he wanted out of the game — a free education. No NHL fame and glory, but a solid job (he's a financial advisor back in Rochester now) and a beautiful family. Oh yeah, his lovely wife, Shelby, is from Tri-Cities as well. Like I always say, success is in the eyes of the beholder.

Another close pal was Chad Cabana, who was our captain. Cabby was a big, tough forward with average skill who just loved to play the game. He kept everybody loose and he thought he and I were always in cahoots, but I'd fuck with him. One game he played awesome but came off early to get his knee seen by Jerry. I heard his name announced over the PA system as the first star, so I skated onto the ice wearing his jersey with a hat pulled down over my eyes so people wouldn't realize who it really was. Back then the first star of the game would have to get interviewed over the loudspeaker for everyone to hear, so I took the mic and guaranteed a fight with Wade Belak in Saskatoon the following week. Then I pumped my own (Cabby's) tires for five minutes or so and hit the showers. The boys all thought this was fantastic, and Cabby laughed it off, but Belak ended up giving him a pretty good shiner a few days later!

There was a healthy team chemistry in Tri-Cities, and I think it was magnified for two reasons. The first was the fact that the legal drinking age there is 21, so we were never in bars. (In Red Deer we all hit the bar from time to time because you can legally drink at 18.) We snuck the odd margarita at Applebee's or Red Lobster, but that was the extent of it. I am not saying we didn't have team get-togethers in which alcohol, music, and ladies were involved, but they were few and far between, well planned, and fairly responsible given the situation. We generally went to school in the mornings and had practice in the early afternoon. We had a lot of fun, and sometimes we had to get creative to break the afternoon boredom, which occurred after school and practice but before we had to be home to our billets for dinner.

Another reason my group there was tight was the fact that a lot of us had to live through the horror of our captain, Todd Klassen, passing away in 1993. He was on the way to Tri-Cities in late July for the annual boat race event, and to get an early start on training, when tragedy struck. Todd was involved in a fatal car accident. We all loved him. As a 15-year-old player, I was brought in by Tri-Cities a few times during the year and always had me stay with him. They wanted me to learn from him. He was a born leader and was drafted by Pittsburgh, with a good shot at playing in the NHL no doubt. The nucleus of our hockey team lived through that and it brought us closer together. We always felt we were in some small way playing for Todd.

Crash Test Dummy

In 1995–96, our team was in second place in our division for much of the season; I had been drafted by the Canadiens the previous summer, and life was good. We had a real tight group of fellas and were in good spirits most of the time. (To us, second place was like first, because Kamloops were so good, winning an unprecedented three Memorial Cups in four years.) Craig Stahl was very immature, much like myself, and we would drive around town entertaining ourselves at other people's expense. The following is a list of just some of the stupid shit we pulled:

1) Wearing only thong underwear and cowboy boots, we hit a movie together—I think it was *Ace Ventura: When Nature Calls*—making everyone around us squeamish, to say the least.

2) We painted black-and-gold stripes down the middle of my Dodge Lancer and wrote the words "Flying Rabbi" on the back, then proceeded to paint the wheels pink and gold.

3) At team autograph signings we would give ourselves different nicknames with each signature, like Terry "the Tornado" Ryan, or Craig "the Killer" Stahl and see which ones turned up at home games (that's where "Flying Rabbi" came from).

4) We dressed up like superheroes and walked into local establishments, claiming we sensed trouble and were offering our services if help was needed.

5) We drove across state lines into Pendleton, Oregon, and walked into a "strip club"—which amounted to a few strung-out women, a bar, and a pole in someone's rec room filled with greasy old dusters who hadn't gotten laid since they got out of jail—and gave out free tickets

for seats behind our bench to anyone who wanted to take in a game (not a good idea).

6) We wrote complaint letters to corporations like Pepsi, Oakley, and Nike. We received tons of free stuff—Colgate even sent us a crate of toothpaste when we said we found hairs inside a tube of their product.

7) We had a bottle of rancid-smelling stuff, I think it was ammonium sulfide. It was what they use to make stink bombs. Anyway, we would open it here and there when everyone was together, like in the room or on the bus. It was such a bad odour, everyone would be pissed off and bickering. The chirps were so funny it was easy to blend our laughter in with everyone else's. We kept that secret for the better part of two years and used it on long bus rides for much-needed entertainment.

8) Tom Zavediuk and Marc Stephan were arguing about who could eat more, and Stahlzy all of a sudden said, "I bet Newf can eat every burger on the McDonald's menu." After the wagers were in, I ate every last burger, and Stahlzy and I used the profits—a whopping $20—to take in a movie. Needless to say, I was extremely full, but I told the boys I was still hungry, and on the way out I grabbed six nuggets and a fries and *forced* it in me, acting like I felt nothing (I really do love a good story).

Luckily, our coach for most of our time in TC, Bob Loucks, had a good sense of humour. He knew that keeping guys loose was part of a good leader's job, and in our own way Stahlzy and I were comical, not criminal. As long as we stayed within the parameters of good taste we had the green light to entertain.

One day, we were all on the ice, dead tired, in the middle of a long practice, and coming off a long road trip. The pace had already begun to slow to midget-hockey level, and guys were getting pissed off at each other during contact drills. Passes were pitiful and shots were all neck-high (when players get pissed off and the team does shooting drills, being a goalie is like being the bull's eye at a shooting range full of deranged snipers). People were annoyed, and Loucksy loved to bag-skate us if we fucked up. I'd be lying if I said I remembered what we did wrong, but we fucked up and were paying the price, bottom line.

All of a sudden, for reasons unbeknownst to us, the fire alarm went off. Someone in the office had pulled it because there was a gas leak in the building, so we had to go outside until professionals were brought in to assess the situation. On the way, I snagged the keys to my car. I have no idea why — we hadn't thought of a plan yet — but I figured my car was out there and if nothing else I could start it up and keep warm. Tri-Cities didn't get a lot of snowy days at all, but as luck would have it, snow and ice covered the ground in all directions. There weren't many salt or sand trucks to help keep roads clear — most people just stayed indoors when the weather acted up.

The pavement was so icy you could skate on it, and that's exactly what a few of us did. Myself, Stahlzy, Lanks, and the Hurley brothers — Mark and Mike — boarded my vehicle to keep warm after racing to it on skates, across a parking lot which, although icy, no doubt had pebbles and rocks littering it and therefore scuffed up our blades. I am quite certain Loucksy was starting to get annoyed because his face was red and his jaw was clenched. I started the car — wearing my skates as shoes — and we waited a few minutes. When the car warmed up I drove closer to where everyone was standing. Now I was sure of it — Loucksy was livid. Not at us in particular, just the whole situation, although me having my car stereo playing "Video Killed the Radio Star" full blast didn't help. And the car we were in was none other than the Flying Rabbi, all glittered up with those stupid stripes running down the middle.

Stahlzy looked at me from the passenger seat as the brothers Hurley and Lanks chatted in the back, and he knew exactly what I was thinking and started to giggle. With that, I took off. Lanks was pissed at first but started to laugh, and even Mark Hurley—the oldest of us four, and a guy who was normally pretty responsible—smiled as our getaway car sped away, blaring the soundtrack of our lives (actually my '80s mix tape). We looked crazy, but on top of all this I used to drive around in a crash test dummy mask and videotape people's reactions (another way Stahlzy and I killed time), so I threw it on.

We were now cruising around TC with our skates on in the middle of winter with '80s music blasting from the fully-lowered windows, being led by an idiot in a crash test dummy mask. We felt overwhelmingly happy and free for around three or four minutes . . . and then realized we should head back. "I know how we will cheer everyone up," I said to the boys. "We'll bring everyone back hot chocolate and coffee." We had just passed a McDonald's and weren't too far from the coliseum, so I pulled a sharp U-turn at full speed and crashed into a protruding snow bank on the other side of the road near the Mickey D's entrance. As we hit the snow bank, the back wheel crashed into the sidewalk hidden underneath and bent inwards from top to bottom, making the car shake as it proceeded.

The drive-thru was crowded, so we all got out of the car and skated in to grab some treats for the gang back at practice, from which we had been absent for what was now a healthy 25 minutes. We ordered a couple of dozen coffees and hot chocolates (and I snagged a cheeseburger as well) and boarded the Flying Rabbi back to hockey practice. We were all excited and laughing again now, figuring the boys would be pumped we were arriving with wintery treats. I made a few quick stops at the odd stoplight and banged my head off the steering wheel like a true crash test dummy and produced some astounded looks from passersby, sending the boys into fits of laughter.

When we got back to practice, the rink just had the feel of negativity. I could sense we were in trouble. The guys were getting skated pretty hard and when we walked through the room en route to the ice, we had to pass Loucksy and he looked pissed! All I remember is a single vein running down the side of his head by the corner of his eye, where the lenses of his glasses met the handles. His face was red, and he yelled something I don't recall, but I know it wasn't good. As we walked, we tracked rocks and mud on the spectacular floor in our dressing room. There was mud all over the Americans logo woven into the carpet. Mike Hurley offered Loucksy a coffee and he grabbed it, apprehensively, and told us to get the hell out onto the ice. We brought out the hot drinks and passed them around as the fellas skated over. They were pissed as well. Loucksy had been punishing them for our fuck-up and now he was even madder because we interrupted his practice. On top of all this, the drinks were freezing cold at this point and therefore useless.

After 10 minutes or so, Loucksy snapped, threw his stick, and skated "Team Hot Chocolate" hard for the rest of practice. We were absolutely bagged. And to make matters worse, some fan called the office and reported seeing "a fool in Terry Ryan's car driving around in a mask, scaring children and creating havoc." It was one of the only times I felt I had truly gone too far, but at practice the next day Loucksy was quick to point out we had to gel if we wanted to win, and from time to time all members of a family fuck up! It's not like we broke the law or anything, but I know where he was coming from. There is a time and a place for everything, and we as players had to respect the coach, GM, and each other. They made us tell the whole story in front of the team and I vividly remember Loucksy crying with laughter.

Bob Loucks, by the way, is one of the best coaches I ever had, and remains a true friend to this day. He was as important to our success in the desert, both as players and as people, as anyone. We appreciate it, Loucksy, and didn't get a chance to say it enough!

The Mike Milbury Story

Edmonton, Alberta: three days before the 1995 NHL Entry Draft. It was beneficial for guys in my league that the draft was held in Edmonton — the WHL had many fans and representatives on hand for reasons of simple geography. Most NHL teams had entire hotel rooms booked for the week, and if you happened to be a draft prospect or player of interest, it was likely that you were going to be interviewed in one of the rooms by the brass. Tri-Cities had numerous players who were draft-eligible, and along with myself at number eight two other guys would also be selected in the first round (Brian Boucher number 21, Daymond Langkow number 5). Three more players would be drafted in later rounds: Pavel Kriz (97), Boyd Olson (138), and Ray Schultz (184). Lanks, Boyd, and Schultzy were from Edmonton, so come draft day we would have a bigger cheering section than most.

I remember doing a lot of the pre-draft stuff with Daymond, maybe because we played on the same line. A few of the "interviews" stand out. New Jersey, for example, was basically a fitness test culminating with the dreaded VO2 max challenge. This test is pretty much mandatory now in most training camps. It is important because it measures the maximum capacity of a player's body to use and transport oxygen during exercise, and this in turn gives one a general sense of the player's physical condition. I considered it torture — you start at a light jog on a treadmill with a tube in your mouth and the machine picks up its grade and speed each minute until finally you are sprinting uphill. You don't jump off until you literally can't go any further. This, for me and many others, meant blurred vision and dizziness. There's healthy competition between players, especially at an event like this, and most guys hold nothing back.

Washington's one-on-one time included interviews that seemed to test IQ and stuff, and if they were seriously interested in picking you they would have likely already flown you down to Washington for more elaborate testing.

Things were getting monotonous, and Lanks and I were in the midst of what seemed like our 100th interview, answering what seemed like our millionth question.

Q: Are you a follower or a leader?

A: I lead by example. The only place *I* comes before *team* is in the dictionary, and I do whatever I have to in order to get that message across to my coaches and teammates.

Q: So, do you drink alcohol?

A: Not really. I have had it a few times if we are together on a bus trip. Team-bonding type of stuff.

Q: Do you have good morals and values, and what are some of your hobbies?

A: Well, I am glad you asked. I would think I do have good values, as I was brought up by great parents. As far as hobbies go, I like to read. In fact, last night I realized I forgot my books at home so I went back to my hotel room and read the Bible again. Did I mention I give 110% every night?

And so on, and so on, and so on. I mean, you are 18 years old, with limited life experience; there's only so much you can add to these answers to spice them up.

I called my agent, Mike Barnett (he was Daymond's agent too). Mike represented Wayne Gretzky and a slew of other superstars, and Lanks and I were fortunate to have that kind of experience on our side. Mike confirmed that I had only two interviews left: one with the New York Islanders, which would be conducted by Mike Milbury, and one with the Tampa Bay Lightning, which would take place with the legendary Phil Esposito. I told him to call the Islanders and tell them I would be right up.

Five minutes later I was at my meeting. I walked in and took a seat at the far end of the table, noticing an empty chair at the other end. All the scouts and team brass were sitting around the table; it was long and oval and gave the place a conference-room feel. These guys seemed to like me and, if I do say so myself, I was doing a better than average job. I hate to act like I wasn't still in awe of the situation, but it was getting hard to answer the same questions over and over every day. The fact that these guys were picking topics I hadn't discussed yet was as exhilarating as a breath of fresh air after leaving a cluttered dressing room during the playoffs.

After what I would guess to be 15 or 20 minutes, the room went silent and I heard footsteps coming in from the adjoining room. The sound of the footsteps started faint and grew louder and louder, until finally there he was. It was the GM of the New York Islanders himself, Mike Milbury. He had a presence about him and immediately started asking the non-sugar-coated questions and throwing out comments I had yet to hear from the other teams. His statements were cloaked in criticism. "You skate faster with the puck than without it," he said first.

"Okay, I never noticed that," I replied.

"And you sure benefitted from playing with Daymond Langkow the whole year," was his next dig.

"Well, I like to think he benefitted from playing with me too, Mr. Milbury," I said with open eyes and a puppy dog look on my face.

"And finally," he said, "I heard you had a good tilt with Wade Belak." Belak was one of the WHL's most feared players and a legitimate heavyweight. He was a great person—and out of my league when it came to fighting. I hung in there with him once that season and never fought him again because the fight legend was gaining momentum and I didn't want to ruin it.

"Do you really think you could do it again?"

I was getting annoyed, but I knew he was testing me. He was a former player and was doing exactly what I would do if I was in the same situation with a young smartass in front of me today. He was getting a feel for me. I was intrigued and accepted his challenge.

"Mr. Milbury, if you don't like me, don't select me. You guys are picking at number one, where I know I am not going. Your next pick is at number 20-something, and I sure as hell know I am not going there. Judging by the Central Scouting ratings, I will probably fall somewhere comfortably in the middle. There is a better guy for you in this draft pool than me, obviously."

The tension was building.

"Okay, kid," he says. "I am going to give you a scenario. Let's say it's 10:50 and you and a buddy have just been out with a couple girls. Your buddy leaves and you are left alone with a beautiful young girl who really digs you. It's a 10-minute drive home and curfew is at 11:00, but she invites you to stay for a few minutes and you know if you do you will get lucky. Remember, it's a 10-minute drive. What do you do, kid?"

I swear to God the answer popped into my head immediately like I had been waiting to hear those words my entire young life.

"Well, Mike," I said, now choosing to drop the "Mr. Milbury" moniker. I took a sip of my bottled water so as to build the suspense. "I fuck her for five minutes and then I speed home!"

I knew it was the end of my meeting anyway, and as I looked around the table, half the scouts were laughing and half were looking at each other in disbelief. I got up and made my way to the door, totally realizing I may have stepped out of line, but in my mind the joke was hilarious and therefore justifiable, so fuck it. And I was right, they weren't realistically going to take me anyway. The comment probably sounded cocky coming from a kid, but I was trying to be witty more than anything. Either way, I am glad I said it, because the story has been good to me over the years, and has always been received with a few laughs. It has come to represent a time in my life I look back on with great fondness—we had the world by the balls without fully realizing it.

Napoleon's Bone

Right after the Milbury interview, I made my way to my last meeting, with hockey legend Phil Esposito, GM of Tampa Bay. It wound up being my favourite meeting of all because of his honesty and the fact that he was a Canadian icon. His brother Tony—one of the best goalies ever—was present as well, so it was all a little surreal.

Hell, the whole week was surreal.

I walked into the room and Espo sat me down and said, "Kid, I heard about the answer you gave in the Islanders meeting . . . funny stuff! By the way, how far apart did Napoleon sleep from his wife?"

"A *Bonaparte*," I answered, again ready for anything.

"Ha! Awesome, kid. Now, I am going to be honest. We are not

looking at taking you at fifth overall, but we are very interested in your pal Daymond Langkow. What can you tell me about him?"

"Well, Mr. Esposito," I started to say, as my answers seemed rehearsed by this point, "he is a hard worker, great shot, tough, great in the dressing room. He is a great fit for any organization, and . . ."

He cut me off.

"Okay, okay, listen Terry, I mean what kind of guy is he? Do you trust him and do you guys hang out? Is he hung up on women? Does he handle pressure well? And by the way, you can call me Espo."

"Espo, the guy is a great friend, hockey or no hockey," I said. "He is trustworthy, from a great family, and his determination to succeed has never been second-guessed by anyone I have known who has spent any time with him during the last three years. He gets along well with his girlfriend, Stephanie — they are both close pals."

"Thanks, kid. The interview is now over, but feel free to hang out with Tony and me for a bit. We can chat a little."

I started with the 1972 Summit Series and must have worn those men out with questions. For the next hour I sat and shot the shit with two guys who were almost 40 years my senior and who had very little in common with me . . . except that we were hockey players. But, of course, that was all we needed. The Lightning ended up taking Daymond with their first pick, fifth overall.

Respect Redden

One of the guys I went through a lot of that pre-draft stuff with was Wade Redden. Wade got picked number two that year, and we played together as 16-year-olds on Team Pacific, an all-star team made up of players from

Alberta and British Columbia, in the World Under-17 tournament. I am not particularly close with him, in fact I barely know the guy today. But you know what is really starting to piss me off? All the Wade Redden–bashing I've heard over the last few years. Granted, the one-time superstar is one of the highest paid guys ever to play in the American Hockey League, and I actually had him on my list of underachievers in the NHL in 2011–12 based on that fact alone. However, Redden seems to be more known nowadays as the butt of a joke in a sports bar near you than for anything else, and I have had enough of it.

The fact is, Redden has had a remarkable career in hockey whichever way you slice it. I get pissed off when fans are so fickle they turn on players who bled for them. And yeah, I'm venting by using Wade Redden as an example. So listen up, all bandwagoners and blabbermouths—the next time you open a beer with a buddy and want to start gossiping about everyone's favourite overpaid minor-leaguer, think about this:

In junior, Redden helped the Brandon Wheat Kings get to two Memorial Cup tournaments (he was named a tournament all-star in 1996). He captured a World Junior Championship gold medal twice, each time contributing mightily to the win. He was chosen as the WHL rookie of the year in 1994, and in his final two years of junior, Wade was named to the all-star team twice and was widely regarded as the most dependable damn defenceman by his peers. He played way older than his years at every level and in 1996 scored a goal on his first shot, versus the Montreal Canadiens. Redden enjoyed a spectacular NHL career by anyone's standards and was a fan favourite in Ottawa for more than a decade as a result of his determined work ethic, strong play, and charitable nature (those who criticize his character are quick to forget projects like "Wade's World," a luxury box paid for by Redden each game from the late '90s until his departure in 2008 and donated to local children who were terminally ill). His on-ice play was rewarded by NHL all-star selections in 2002 and 2004, and in 2006 Wade led the NHL in plus/minus, finishing with a staggering plus-35 rating. In 2007, Redden and the rest of the Senators came close to bringing Canada its first Stanley Cup Championship title since the Habs won it all in 1993; they lost the final in five games to Anaheim's Ducks but gained respect throughout the hockey world for their strong playoff performance.

As for international hockey accolades as a pro? In 1999 and 2001, Mr. Redden was selected to play for Canada at the World Hockey Championships, but the team fell short in their efforts to win gold. In 2005 he finally took home a silver medal from the Worlds, losing to the Czech Republic in the final. Although our standards here in Canada are overwhelmingly high when it comes to winning and hockey — usually we only have space in our papers for "golden" stories — this doesn't change the accomplishment or the fact that Redden answered the bell for his country. Not everybody does. In Italy in 2006, Canada's Olympic hockey squad was shockingly left off the podium, but again Redden was on the team and played well at the Games. We all rooted for him. To top all this off, Redden won a World Cup of Hockey with Canada in 2004 and injured himself in the process, laying it all on the line for his country in order to get a job done. His presence in the locker room is often sought after, and this is evidenced by the many captain's *C*'s and *A*'s he has worn proudly on his chest throughout his career.

Yes, Wade Redden is overpaid now, as his career draws to a close, but that isn't entirely his fault. The Rangers signed him to the deal. Ask any player, they aren't going to turn down a payday, especially near the end of a long career. He was set to earn top dollar on the free market either way, whether it was with the Rangers or one of the other teams bidding for his services at the time. I understand the hockey world may be presently down on him—so be it. But I think people are conveniently forgetting about his achievements. Things like what entertaining hockey he brought us and what a great humanitarian he can be. I can think of many players who played less, and achieved less, and who take nowhere near the amount of abuse this guy gets. Is he going to return to form? Probably not! The guy is 35 now. Has he earned his coin from NYC? God, no! But the fact remains, at this point Wade Redden does not have to justify his hockey abilities to anyone. His career falls somewhere between NHL "regular" and Hall of Fame candidate, in my opinion, and if I were Wade I'd be very happy with my place in the game.

How am I so sure about his character? Well, we were drafted in the same year ('95) and you get to know your peers during that time. I don't mind saying that he was the best player on Team Pacific in 1994, as well as our best leader in the room. I remember Wade as being very quiet, but when he spoke everyone listened. In three years playing as his opponent in junior, I saw night in and night out how superb he was at what he did, which was play with smooth poise and deceptive skills in an effortless, almost flawless manner. Nothing flashy, but always solid. He always made the right play.

I haven't spoken to Wade since the night he scored his first NHL goal in 1996 in Montreal. I was with the Canadiens, standing outside our locker area as he was getting whisked away from his dressing room towards the *Hockey Night in Canada* headquarters for a well-deserved post-game interview. We were still very aware of each other and I remember seeing him smile when I shook his hand and we spoke briefly. At that point, professional hockey is fresh and surreal, and each day seems like a dream. I don't recall everything we talked about, but I know that as a former teammate of his, I felt proud that evening because of his first big-league tally. That was over 15 years ago, and if I saw him now, I think I would say the same thing I said then: "Great job, and good luck in the future, buddy."[1]

Hey Now, You're An All-Star

As far as my junior hockey career goes, if there was a peak it had to be the 1995 CHL all-star game in Kitchener, Ontario.

The 1994–95 season was a lockout year — the first of three during Gary Bettman's tenure as league commissioner so far — which made it all the more unlikely that myself and Daymond would play in the all-star game. The NHL had just resumed play, but all year we were battling for statistics with junior players who would otherwise be in the NHL, like Rob Niedermayer, Ryan Smyth, and Jeff Friesen. You see, in 1996, the CHL started an annual prospects game, designed to show off the best players the CHL had to offer in the upcoming NHL Entry Draft. However, from 1992 to 1995, the event was labelled the CHL "All Star Challenge" and featured the best players from the WHL, OHL, and QMJHL, no matter what age. With this system, it was much harder to make the cut as a draft-eligible player, because there were players up to three years older. From the WHL that year, the only draft-eligible guys to make the team were myself, Lanks, and Wade Redden. Lanks was leading the WHL in scoring, and I was his fearless

---

1 I'll point out that since I wrote this story in early 2012, Wade Redden played for the St. Louis Blues and the Boston Bruins in the 2012–13 season. The Bruins, who made it to within one game of winning the Stanley Cup, acquired his services for the playoff run, and he was playing great before getting hurt after just six games. He helped the team in a big way, providing solid play with invaluable experience. The series he played most in, versus the Leafs, was a seven-game battle for the ages. Told you so.

sidekick, also in the top five in that category, so it was hard to deny us the gig. Redden was rated to go first or second in the draft and was dominant, so he was a shoo-in. What made it even more difficult was the way they picked the teams. One league would host and the other two would combine. The game was in Kitchener, so the OHL made up the home team, and the WHL and QMJHL formed the other team. So there were only 10 guys — of any age under 21 — taken from our league. Future stars like Jarome Iginla and Shane Doan — also in their draft years — didn't make the cut, so it was elite company indeed, and a thrill to be selected. My guess is I barely made the squad. I was a virtual unknown compared to the other stars selected for the game, guys like Darcy Tucker, Eric Daze, Martin Biron, Jeff O'Neill, Todd Bertuzzi, and Bryan Berard, just to name a few.

The whole experience was surreal. My dad flew up from the Rock to meet me, and I never usually got to see my parents during the season, so it was a welcome surprise. As I mentioned before, my agent was Mike Barnett and he represented the Great One himself, so on the way to the game he and Mike and my dad stopped in to Wayne's childhood home in Brantford, Ontario, and met with Mr. and Mrs. Gretzky. We still have the pic on our wall at home, with TR Senior posing in front of Wayne's old hockey trophies.

Before the game, I must admit, I was intimidated when I looked at all the talent around the room. Bryan McCabe sat next to me — he was an archrival with the Spokane Chiefs back in the WHL, and he had recently won a World Junior gold medal in Red Deer (even though Lanks and I had great years, there was no way we were making that Team Canada squad; we were inexperienced, and many players on the team — including 1993 first-overall pick Alexandre Daigle — would have been in the NHL had it not been for the lockout), and I had a chat with him as we put on our gear for the warm-up/photo-op. He was a nice guy, even though I kinda wanted to hate him because of our circumstances back in the WHL. I knew he was only two years older than me, but he seemed 30 at the time, just removed from not only winning the WJC but being selected as a tournament all-star.

A few more of the boys piped up and started some dressing room banter, and things became more relaxed from my side. I started yappin' and told a few stories — a couple of which are in this book — and within minutes the atmosphere was as loud as a post-game beer-league dressing room in holiday season. Most of these dudes knew each other already from NHL camps or tournaments like the WJC, so it didn't take long to gel. Before we hit the ice, our captain, Marty Murray, gave us a pep talk not unlike others he'd given so many times in Brandon, Manitoba, as a member of the Wheat Kings — and away we went.

For whatever reason, it felt like we were "in the zone" immediately. Even in warm-up, I had that great feeling — it happens rarely, but when it does you feel like you can do nothing wrong. I should have been ultra-nervous, as is normally the case, but I think that because the expectations were so low, it was impossible to fuck up too bad, and any positive impact Lanks or I had would be considered a bonus. Even though we were both having great seasons, we were at the low end of the totem pole in a group like this. I'm not taking anything away from Daymond Langkow or myself; all I'm saying is that the year before, we'd had modest seasons, to say the least, and our current success was only months old. Also, the CHL teams based in the USA tend to get less attention than the Canadian teams, especially Tri-Cities. I loved it there, but it was off the radar as far as attention from Canadian media goes. We never saw any Canadian TV cameras at our games during my time there, without exception. When I got traded to hockey hotbed Red Deer in 1997, my second game with the Rebels was televised nationwide. Go figure.

We got off to a great start and didn't look back. Our coach was Don Hay, and as the head coach of the Kamloops Blazers he coached against Lanks and me back in the West Division of the WHL. He put us on the same line (no surprise) and threw Frederic Chartier—a 50-goal-scorer for Laval—on our right side. Frederic was also a lesser-known player in that game and couldn't have been a better fit. We skated hard, hit everything we could, and were rewarded for our efforts. I can't remember the exact score, but after the first period our team was ahead and Lanks and I both had goals, with Freddy C gathering assists on both. A couple of points for all three of us. In the dressing room after the initial period, I was pumped. I knew we were opening a few eyes . . . but what now? I had a plan . . .

As we got ready to start the second frame, I looked at Lanks on the bench and told him I was going to go ask Ed Jovanovski to drop the mitts. Jovo had gone number one overall the year before, in 1994, and was a superstar junior player for the Windsor Spitfires of the OHL and also played on that superb '95 World Junior Team Canada. The way I saw it, I'd already had an impact on the game (I'd never in my wildest dreams expected to score a goal, and I already had a goal and an assist) and completing the "Gordie Howe hat trick" (one goal, one assist, one fight) would surely turn some heads and snag me a higher ranking in the upcoming NHL draft that summer. I knew my agent and father—who were familiar with my thought process—wouldn't be surprised at my actions if I chose to start a scrap in the prestigious all-star game, but just about everyone else in the crowd would be. It'd get people talking!

As I jumped on the ice for my first shift of the second period, I dumped the puck into Jovo's corner of the ice and started striding like a bat outta hell towards the dangerous hitter, only to be knocked on my ass convincingly. I got up and was gonna ask him to go but tripped over my stick, which had fallen to the ice. Shit. All that adrenaline and build-up for nothing.

I skated back into our zone and looked around the ice, ready to go back on the attack. I was actually caught out of position because I was behind the play, cheating on the offensive side, and the puck all of a sudden came right to me as I swung into the middle of the ice in our own end. When I took control of the puck and looked up, I saw one defender between me and the opposite goal, and I was still in my own end of the rink. The defender was fellow Atlantic-Canadian David Ling, and he was out of position. Linger was a forward and was covering for future Maple Leafs pick Jeff Ware, the defenceman who normally would have been there. When I realized this, I saw my opportunity and took advantage of it.

I was in full stride and made a quick deke on Linger, who had just started retreating backwards and would have had to make a sensational play to stop me. It must have looked like I was a fast as a bullet out there, given the circumstances, but in reality all the stars had aligned and the situation couldn't have been any more perfect. After the deke on Linger, I only had OHL standout goalie Dan Cloutier to beat, and beat him I did. Like a rented mule, as legendary Pittsburgh Penguins broadcaster Mike Lange would say. Cloutier was a phenomenal goalie in junior who starred for the OHL's Sault Ste. Marie Greyhounds, so it made the moment extra-cool. I looked right but tucked the puck up under the left bar on his blocker side—my best goal of the year, hands down, and arguably the best-looking goal of my junior career.

I figure the chances of this happening were astronomically low. I mean, what a time to have a game like this—on national television, amongst all these future stars. Had my career ended right there, it would have ended with a huge smile, I'll tell you that. I acted all cool after the goal, but when I got to the bench I looked at Lanks and nearly hyperventilated! He couldn't believe it either. We smiled and bit our lips, but we knew we were raising eyebrows. Three points each. Halfway through.

"Okay, Lanks, nothing fancy. Safe plays for the rest of the game and we're sittin' pretty!" I said with a laugh.

"Whatever you say, Newf," Lanks replied. (Anyone who has played with Daymond Langkow knows he is a man of few words at times but does his leading by example. He actually was great at making me feel comfortable, because he has nerves of steel and rarely gets rattled — if at all. It was no doubt one of the reasons I felt so at ease on that particular evening.)

I'd love to say we both ended up with more goals, but things cooled off after that. Later in the second period, however, I got hammered hard in the corner by Bryan Berard — the guy was my age and rated number one in the world — so I said fuck it and dropped the gloves with him instead. Ironically, we were both represented by Mike Barnett, so my father was actually sitting with Mr. Berard! To his credit, the younger Berard responded right away and we had a very spirited bout right in front of Team OHL's net. I got him with a few more punches, but he threw me down at the end. The fans cheered, we winked at each other, and as we skated to the penalty box I started to soak in everything that just happened. I had scored two goals and an assist and had a great fight, and we still had a period to go. In the all-star game. Nobody fights in the all-star game! I'm not sure how many fights there have been, but I am sure they have been few and far between. I know there have been a couple in the prospects game, but that is an entirely different situation. Prospects are battling for ranking, but we had been playing a game that had historically been a non-fighting affair.

The game ended after an average third period for me and Lanks, but the seed had been planted. We had shown our stuff to the hockey world, and our stock was rising, fast. I was chosen as player of the game by a few media outlets—including RDS, a French-language sports station in Quebec—and TSN's Gord Miller gave me the post-game interview. I laughed and smiled the whole time! I wasn't only happy because I had a good game, but it actually felt good to be close to home. I know, I know, Kitchener is far from Newfoundland . . . but as I mentioned before, in Tri-Cities we were not only as far away in North America geographically as we could be from my hometown, we didn't get much press outside of Kennewick. Many people in Newfoundland hadn't seen me play much, and many others questioned my parents for moving me away at such a young age. I felt vindicated, for them, myself, and everyone who believed in me.

Oh, and my favourite part of the story is that when I met David Ling a couple of years later, we were lining up against each other for a faceoff at Montreal camp, and he says, "Hey TR, let's go for a beer after. You're paying, and you owe me half of your contract, asshole! I let you go around me in the all-star game!" I burst out laughing on the ice. We ended up being linemates that season in Fredericton and have been close ever since.

For what it's worth, I think the fact that Lanks and I performed so well changed the whole process of how they play the annual game now. There were other draft-eligible players in the game who were great prospects and had good games as well, like Jason Doig on our side and Marc Savard and Alyn McCauley on the other. Wade Redden played his usual solid game. I mean, think about it—the next season they canned the CHL All-Star Challenge in favour of a prospects game. One would have to think our success as younger players who nearly didn't make the cut had to play at least a small role in the format change. Who knows, maybe I'm dead wrong . . . but maybe I'm not. If there is some small truth to my opinion, however, it makes me even happier about that unbelievable night in late January 1995, because it would mean we as a group helped the circumstances of other prospects who came after us.

Either way, that particular game was probably the highlight of my junior hockey career — at least on a personal level — and getting to experience it in Canada, with my good buddy at my side, only added icing to the cake.

It's All for Rebel

As long as I am talking about junior hockey and tough Indians, I might as well get into my experience with the Red Deer Rebels by telling you a bit about one of my best buddies in the game, Arron Asham.

Ash played the 2012–2013 season with the New York Rangers hockey club, and has made a career out of being one of the best grinders in the league. Ash has played in the NHL for over a decade now (I say this like a proud big brother) and, pound for pound, is one of the toughest fighters of his era. If you hit one of his teammates with a cheap shot, get ready for a tap on the shoulder and an invitation to the dance floor. Arron isn't putting on a show out there — he is as pugilistic off the ice as he is on it. He's not one to instigate a confrontation, but if you rub him the wrong way it's go time.

One of the things people forget about the man some call the Little Ball of Hate is how talented he is as a hockey player. Ash had back-to-back seasons of 40-plus goals while playing a starring role for the Red Deer Rebels in the late 1990s, and he even cracked the national Under-18 team in his draft year. He's a great player to have for depth purposes because he doesn't command a huge salary but can play a lot of roles. If a first- or second-liner goes down with an injury, Ash has the skills to fill that void, and not all role players can do that. He listens to his coaches, which obviously helps his cause. Ash and I played together in junior and shared the experience of being prospects in the Habs system for a few years; we were pretty close pals in those days.

The first time I played against Arron, he was a 16-year-old rookie with the Red Deer Rebels. I was 17, enjoying my breakthrough year as a fourth-year junior about to get drafted. He asked me to fight twice a shift for the whole game. He called me every name in the book. It's not that I was scared of the Little Ball of Hate, but I heard that shit a lot that year and I had to pick my spots; the team relied on me to score, and I also played under a lit fuse, so keeping away from foul-mouthed rookies was a must unless they did something stupid. Arron is actually a pretty fair player, so he never did anything stupid, but on the way off the ice after the game, he threw a water bottle at me and called me a gutless chickenshit. I laughed, and most of what I know about Arron's athletic side can be summed up by those few actions. He is rough around the edges, but he'll do what it takes to be noticed and succeed. He always puts the team first and never complains about ice time. I liked it and was thrilled to see Montreal select him in 1996 in the third round, 71st overall.

In 1996–97, my last year of junior hockey, I was a deadline deal from Tri-Cities to Arron's club, the Red Deer Rebels (we knew each other by now because we'd been roommates at Habs camp the previous autumn). I got traded for prospects, and I believe that's pretty much the norm in junior hockey—if a team is not going to make the playoffs and they have some impact players who are 19 or 20, they trade the big guns to ensure themselves some stability in the future by rebuilding around a new group of young talent. It's part of the normal cyclical pattern that defines junior hockey and is another reason having a consistent junior team is a difficult task. I was actually playing in Montreal that season, having made the team out of camp—I played four games in 1996 as a 19-year-old—but had some post-concussion syndrome symptoms from a big hit early on. By the time the junior trade deadline rolled around, I'd been symptom-free for a month. GM Rejean Houle called me into his office and told me my junior rights were now owned by the Red Deer Rebels; I was leaving in the morning, and good luck in our quest for the Memorial Cup, he said.

I was so excited! I knew Red Deer had a good squad and were going to be a force in the Eastern Division. My old Tri-Cities buddy BJ Young played for the Rebels now too, so the couple of guys I knew there were "salt o' the earth," as they say here on the Rock, and that eased the anxiety of joining a new team. I also welcomed the change of pace—the desert was a great place to play junior, but Red Deer seemed to be closer to the nucleus of the hockey world.

In fact, in three years of playing for a team full of prospects in Tri-Cities, we never had one game on Canadian television. A few games against Seattle or Portland (fairly big markets when compared with Moose Jaw and Prince Albert) were broadcast on northwest U.S. channels, but most Canadian junior hockey fans only knew our team name by reading it in the *Hockey News*. The Canadian teams tend to get more coverage; in my second game as a Red Deer Rebel in late January 1997, we played the Brandon Wheat Kings in a regular season game and blew them out 7–2. It was broadcast on TSN and was the first time people watching from the Rock had seen me play a game in the WHL. (I had five points and slid down the ice on my knees after a goal, pumping my fists in the air like a maniac. It was a hot-dog move, but I was pumped to be back playing and contributing).

We went all the way to the Eastern Division final that season before running into a fantastic Lethbridge Hurricanes squad that beat us with the likes of Chris Phillips, Shane Willis, Byron Ritchie, and Bryce Salvador leading their ship, amongst some underrated juniors, like 43-goal sniper Travis Brigley and crazy/tough Dale Purinton, who told me he was gonna knock out my teeth and wear them for a necklace after the series. (Dale and I played hard against each other but always bought each other a beer after the game. Even in the pros, he was a loon, but there was something likable in his honest approach; the unapologetic barbarity in his demeanour on the ice was oddly appealing.)

Arron and I became good friends, and even though our team lost in the East Division finals, everyone gained some experience — we had our backs to the wall a lot and fought hard together. BJ became the Rebels' single-season goal-scoring record holder by finishing with an astounding 58 snipes — 26 of which came in the 16 regular season games we spent as linemates (we knew each other well on the ice from our Tri-Cities days), so I felt like a big part of that accomplishment. The record still stands and it will always unite us, bringing Tison and me closer by extension. It represents a time when Tison's two fathers worked together to make something magical happen. BJ and I were dynamite together, there's no other way to put it. He was drafted that summer in the sixth round after being overlooked the previous two years, which very seldom happens.

Arron blossomed into an NHL blue-chip prospect after a solid regular season (45 goals, 96 points, 149 PIMs) and signed with Montreal as a result. Our captain and future Rebels coach, Jesse Wallin, was named one of Detroit's top prospects (he would later win a Cup with the team) and captained Canada's World Junior team that year. Big Mike Brown was taken the following summer in the first round of the NHL draft, and for much of that playoff run there was a buzz in central Alberta that didn't focus on the Flames or Oilers.

The Rebels won the Memorial Cup in 2001, and even though the only common denominator with our 1997 team was Justin Mapletoft—a prolific scoring junior who carved out a nice career playing professionally in Europe—I feel we had something to do with that championship because we were the first team in Rebels history that went on a huge playoff run and garnered a lot of outside interest from the hockey world.

One thing that pisses me off, though, is that BJ's jersey isn't retired at what is now called the Enmax Centrium, the site of the team's home games. Not only did the man set a significant record as a member of the Rebels, he also died a tragic death and his son still attends games. This isn't some dude who merely participated in a few games; we are talking about the biggest sniper in the history of the franchise. As I mentioned, Tison is 14 now, and I am proud to have him as a son—he is as much my son as Penny-Laine is my daughter—and it hurts me to see no memory of his biological father in that arena. We spend a lot of time in Red Deer, and it's just not right after all he has been through and all that his father accomplished with the team. I am sure it's an oversight—the Rebels are run by great people—but if any of you read this, please, make things right.

The Hot Stick

I had a lot of fun in junior, and I was fortunate to play on teams that had a few other clowns as well. I am sure my ex-teammates will laugh while reading some of these stories, wondering why I am leaving so many things out — every day was an adventure for many of us. When I got to Red Deer, Ash and BJ had already told the boys about some of our shenanigans, so I felt the need to impress.

The first day I walked in the room I was greeted by Dave "Radar" Horning, who had been my trainer on Team Pacific at the Under-17 World Championships in northern Quebec a few years before. It was good to see a familiar face right off the bat, and a fantastic guy to boot. Radar and I got along well and had the same taste in music. Head coach Rick Carriere and his assistant Doug Hobson sat me down, welcomed me to the Deer, and shot the shit a little before giving me a list of team rules. Captain Jesse Wallin was next; he's the type of guy who oozes leadership and commands respect, and it was clear to me it was his ship and he ran it well. I was led to my stall by BJ and introduced to my stall neighbour, Lloyd Shaw, who had given me a few beatings back in my days with the Americans. One night in Seattle, Lloyd and I had fought to a draw — both of us bleeding from our orbital region — and left the ice to a standing ovation. Shawsy was a few inches taller than me and had about 20 pounds on me. When he hit, it fuckin' hurt. "Glad to have you on my side," I said, and we chatted about past altercations until practice started, breaking the ice nicely.

By the time we were all done showering a few hours later, I was told my roomie would be Scott Burt and I'd be staying with Neil and Vera Tomalty, who had a great family and lived on a big piece of land just outside city limits. They had a huge downstairs with a big screen TV and a pool table, and outside was a giant patio with a hot tub. They were great people; they didn't complain when I fucked up one of their Ski-Doos on a joyride, and they never told Rick after they caught me and Scotty boozing one night. They told us to tell him ourselves, and we did. Rick Carriere said that even though Scotty and I were 19, it wasn't right to put our billets in a hard situation and it didn't set a good example for the team. We got fined. Rick was 100 percent correct, and from then on in we let him know about everything that went down. If we wanted to have a team get-together, he was to know, or else it wouldn't happen, and it worked out fine. Some stuff was outlandish, but he and Doug had a way of taking care of things, and in the end we respected him enough to play by the rules—though on occasion we'd bend them a bit.

My first home game as a Rebel was great; we beat Prince Albert in overtime, and I got credit for the goal. BJ actually scored, but it looked like it bounced off me. He didn't want it changed because he was pumped for me to be contributing right away. It was a very unselfish move; he was clipping along at a good pace—he would end up setting the franchise record for goals that season—and the goal meant more to him than me. Coach Carriere looked like a genius. BJ, Greg Schmidt, and I each tallied five points; we clicked as a line right from the start, and he rewarded the team for a week's worth of hard work by giving all of us a late curfew and a day off.

We all agreed we'd meet in a half an hour at a party we'd been invited to, and the youngest guys would drive because they wouldn't be drinking. I told the boys I'd buy the booze. In my mind I'd already made a lot of money playing a few games in the NHL, and the least I could do was buy a few beers. When I showed up at the party, I was wearing only my snakeskin cowboy boots, a set of bikini briefs, and a cowboy hat, with 24 beers tucked up under my arm. My truck was parked outside, and I had 30 dozen for the party. Within minutes of entering this stranger's house, I had my briefs off and it was naked hoedown time. I brought my stereo and was now DJing the party and loving life. A few of the boys geared down as well, and let's just say no beer was wasted and all the bedrooms were occupied that evening. We all made it home on time, and no harm was done. Scotty and I got home and cracked a few more beers, talking about our epic evening and where we'd all end up in the future. Being a 19- or 20-year-old in major junior comes with a certain amount of suspense; the next season is the start of your life as a pro, university student, or ex-player. The future is uncertain, so nights like that become even more appreciated as you feel it all coming to an end.

As the regular season neared its close, we were playing great. I'd be lying if I said I could remember our exact record in those final 16 regular season games, but I know we won way more than we lost. I proved to be a good fit and stayed on the same line, collecting 35 points and only 10 penalty minutes in those games. That is a huge total, and that's what I needed to get my game back to where it needed to be psychologically; I needed to have some success, and I needed to be concussion-free. I had other people to mix it up for me in Red Deer — it remains the only hockey team I have ever played for that I never fought as a member of. In 32 total games in Red Deer, I scored 31 goals, including 18 in 16 playoff games. My confidence needed the boost!

We were real tough, with heavyweights like Mike Brown, Devin Francon, Lance Ward, Lloyd Shaw, and Stephen Peat — who was only 16 and already one of the toughest players in the league. Ash was a middleweight but was arguably tougher than the heavies — and definitely crazier. He has no fear at all, which can be scary for the opposition and adds to his value as a player (another reason I am not surprised by his NHL longevity). Our goalies were from different worlds: Mike Whitney was 18, often late for the bus, ate whatever he liked, and got into fights on the ice; Marc Magliarditi was an over-ager (at 20) who was very punctual, athletic-looking and sportsmanlike. It turned out to be a good thing, as they brought out the best in each other. Sixteen-year-old Cam Ondrik was our third-stringer, but he was young and learning and would move on to become a starter for Medicine Hat and then Saskatoon shortly afterwards.

Our record at home was stellar, and a bunch of us clowns would always try to outdo each other when it came to goal celebrations. I had been known for ridiculous goal cellys in Tri-City and once caused a brawl by doin' the "canoe" right by Tacoma's bench after an empty net goal; I skated hard for a few strides and then jumped in the air, landing on my ass and gliding down the ice on my rear end, using my Koho Revolution to simulate oars on a boat. BJ, Ash, Schimdty, Brad Leeb, Scotty Burt — pretty much everyone got in on the act in the Deer, and if one of us happened to be honoured with one of game's three stars, we'd try to come up with an original move and put a name on it, hoping it would catch on. I had many bizarre moves, and if the score was out of hand I'd let them fly and piss the whole other team off in the process. The thing is, I always did it for the fans. I never did it on the road (as Alex Ovechkin did, for example, when he got his 50th goal in 2009), because it wasn't about me, and I never did it when the game was close, because something like that can backfire and put the team in a bad position, and if the other team comes back you look like a fuckin' fool. One game stands out to me in particular: BJ nabbed third star and did the "Blind Man" (he waved his stick in front of him like a cane) and got some heat for it, but we laughed because it was pretty funny and he meant no harm by it. Ash received star number two and rode his stick à la Dave "Tiger" Williams while wearing a cowboy hat for good measure, sending the cowboy crowd roaring with delight. Then it was my turn. All the guys came out of the room because everyone got a kick out of seeing us stroke our egos by going wild and getting the fans loud and on their feet. The fans now knew something was in store, as this post-game ritual had gained momentum and had developed its own rhythm. "You're up, Newf," said Andy Nowicki, a plump, friendly fellow who earned some coin coaching our goalies. "Give 'em shit, buddy!"

What I did next became part of the team's folklore. After hearing my name called as the first star of the game, I slowly skated onto the ice with my hands in the air, my stick gripped tightly in my right hand, and removed my bucket with my left hand. I flipped it off and let it bounce off the ice as the fans went crazy, jumping on their seats. I threw the stick to the ice and tossed my gloves aside, getting down onto my knees and rubbing my hands together over the hot stick, seemingly warming them up in the process. As I rubbed and rubbed, my head turned slowly up with my eyes appearing to direct the flames. I looked like the Undertaker. Eventually I looked straight at the ceiling and extended my arms, closing my eyes and feeling the power, symbolizing a religious experience that flirted with the idea of Divine Intervention. The fans loved it, I loved the attention, and it was dubbed the "Hot Stick" in local circles.

I know what you're thinking now. You're thinking this sounds an awful lot like Alex Ovechkin's move back in 2009, the one that was the topic of sports shows everywhere for a few weeks and stands out as the goal celebration of the last decade or so. And it is. The thing is, I am pretty sure he got it from me. It may have been indirectly, but he did. I know this is a huge, preposterous-sounding claim, but it's true. I don't know if he'd ever admit it, but there's a common denominator here—and his name is Jose Theodore. You see, I played three seasons with Theo in Montreal/Fredericton, and we were good pals. Theo was playing for the Washington Capitals at the time Ovie made all this relevant, and unless this is all a huge coincidence, that's where Ovie came up with the move. Whenever Jose and I would stay on the ice for extra work with some of the other prospects, we'd horse around like we did back in Red Deer.

Theo loved the Hot Stick move and another I used to do in Freddy called the "Fisherman," which caused good ol' Rocky Thompson to more or less put a bounty on me one game against the Saint John Flames. Rock was good enough not to brawl me (although he would if he had to) because we were pals from our days in the WHL, but another big tough dude ended up bloodying my nose that night — Matty O'Dette, a big southpaw, 6-foot-5, 230 pounds, who always proved a crowd-pleasing combatant for me; we fought just about every game we ever played and most were punch-for-punch slugfests. I scored on the empty net, took three strides towards centre ice and cast my stick out like a fishing rod, and when it was extended I pulled back two or three times as if to have a bite, and then David Ling threw me the puck like I had caught a fish! Fuckin' hilarious but uncalled for in pro, and I learned my lesson — to a degree.

The morning after Alexander the Great mimicked me on TV, I watched the highlights with Tison from Danielle's couch in Red Deer. I couldn't believe it! Ty was only nine years old and I had only recently become a major part of his life, so he thought for sure I was bullshitting; he thought I was trying to butter him up with stories about me and his late biological father, and I couldn't blame him — I would have thought my story to be a little unrealistic as well! Luckily for me, Jeff Marek — then with CBC and now with Sportsnet — followed junior hockey very closely back in the day, and he remembered me doing the whole thing in Red Deer. He hosted a program on *Hockey Night in Canada* satellite radio and had me on, live in Toronto, just a few days later. I had a great time and we chatted like old buddies. It's an odd way to be remembered, but all my pals home on the Rock still get a kick out of that one, and many people associate my name with that fact alone. Fine by me.

Oh, yeah—for what it's worth, my "Hot Stick" kicked the shit out of Ovie's.

Opportunity Knocks

Hockey is the coolest game on earth—for many reasons. But one of the most important is that it gives a lot of kids a lot of opportunities. If you play junior or NCAA and are fortunate enough to get drafted and make the NHL, that's great. But if we're being realistic, for most players the chances are slim at best. Now, remember those three little words our parents and teachers were always repeating? Stay in school. Every major junior and collegiate player has the opportunity to get their education paid for, and that's a great thing the game gives back. Many people don't realize that choosing the major junior route can still pay for a college education, but it can. Most of the hockey teams in Canadian university hockey are made up of ex-major-junior players who are receiving a free education. And as for the females, there are many opportunities to land a scholarship playing at a North American university—way more than there were when I was a teenager—and our Canadian players continue to fill rosters on both sides of the border. Free travel is also a major perk for a young athlete. From junior hockey to the lowest rungs of pro to the NHL to the Olympics, us small-town Canadians who grew up on farms, fishing villages, mill towns—wherever—get free travel. I encourage any young player to take advantage of the opportunity to get paid to play overseas, because not only is it a great way to gain worldly knowledge but it is a rewarding payoff for all those thousands of dollars moms and dads put towards a child to get through minor hockey (thousands per year for the better part of a decade). Sometimes you don't realize how fortunate you are until it's time to come home, get a real job, and talk about the buddies you may have on *Hockey Night in Canada*. From Anchorage to Augusta, from Toronto to Torino, from Helsinki to Hamburg to Hong Kong, there is a Canadian professional hockey player sipping a cold beer after a game. And he (or she) is loving every minute of it.

Montreal/Freddy Beach
1995–99

The Day I Fought Tie Domi

"If I ever play against Tie fucking Domi, I'll challenge him to a fight. Put money on it."

— Terry Ryan, August 1995

In the late summer of 1995, a few of my buddies and I were hanging out at our good pal Blair "Bonk" Connolly's house in Mount Pearl. Our pal Chris Peddigrew was leaving the island the next day for some reason or another, and he'd be gone awhile. We were having a few beers to say goodbye—the thought of casually drinking in the afternoon was new, and liberating at that—and telling stories on his newly built deck as the last truly hot rays of August sunshine fell upon us. We were all 18 or 19, and my friends had just finished high school and were preparing for the next step, which was moving to the mainland for the purposes of university, work, or a few years of fun.

This is the custom when you come from a thinly populated island with limited employment options on the easternmost edge of a massive country. In the 1990s Newfoundland's economy struggled, because of the cod moratorium more than anything else, and as a result many young people migrated outward to places like Fort McMurray, Alberta, or Guelph, Ontario. At the same time, many Newfoundlanders moved away for a while after high school if they wanted to attend university or travel for a few years and spread their wings a little. One of the main destinations was Toronto, and a few of the guys on the deck involved in our conversation, including Blair, were soon going to be moving to the big city of T-Dot. The boys were excited and joked about getting free tickets to a Leafs game should I make the Habs. I reminded them that I had just been drafted a couple of months earlier, and that no 18-year-old ever makes the Canadiens — it just doesn't happen. I remember saying I would be surprised if I stuck around main camp more than a few days.

As the cold ones flowed and the steaks sizzled on the barbecue, the chat became more interesting and gravitated towards hockey, as was often the case. I was still very much mesmerized by the thought of even skating one shift in the NHL. I hadn't even been to a camp yet — and none of us seemed comfortable with my newly found status as a celebrity of sorts, drafted to arguably the most storied sports franchise on the planet. All of our lives were about to undergo major changes, and mine would be impacted in the most surreal of ways, trying out for a hockey team with and against some of my childhood idols.

"Who do you think is the toughest player in the NHL, T Bone?" said Jeremy "J-Rock" Hart, who was a huge Habs fan and good buddy from my dad's hometown of Grand Falls. (Jeremy and I are still real close, and he is currently one of the head Labatt reps in the province. I've had many free beers on his tab over the years.) My favourite tough guy of all time had been Chris Nilan because he played for the Habs (I grew up cheering for the Canadiens), but J-Rock was asking me who I thought was the toughest player overall in the game at that specific time.

My answer was Bob Probert. Bobby P played in front of some of the most exuberant fans in all of hockey at Joe Louis Arena, night in and night out, and answered the bell whenever he was called upon, and that usually meant being franchise player Stevie Yzerman's policeman. He personified the blue-collar city of Detroit with his pugilistic style and determination, and the character he displayed sticking up for his teammates was admirable even to a non-hockey fan. Years later, after Probie's substance abuse problems became public, it is even more amazing he remained so great at playing the enforcer's role for as long as he did — and being the best at it, hands down. His early death was nothing short of tragic — the man was loved by all who came across him.

But Blair was a huge Leafs fan and had no time for my answer. He thought Tie Domi was far and away the toughest player in the National Hockey League and called Probert a has-been. This didn't sit well with me, and as we went on and on, reciting junior stats and comparing mental notes, Blair said, "Why don't you fight both of them, you dummy, and see who beats you up worse!"

The boys all laughed.

But I responded: "Sure, fuck it. I promise you assholes, if I ever play against Tie fucking Domi, I'll challenge him to a fight. Put money on it." I had no idea about how much actual truth lay behind that drunken promise.

Fast forward a month and a half. There I was, getting ready for warm-up in Maple Leaf Gardens—which, along with the Montreal Forum and Boston Garden, was a hockey shrine about to be torn down to make way for a new breed of sports arenas that would cater to the corporate crew, snub the lower classes, and make the "Jumbotron" part of our everyday vocabulary. Soon there'd be fewer true fans and more "suits" in the crowd. I gotta say, that always pissed me off. The more our sport forges ahead into a new hockey era, the more distance is created between the on-ice product and the true hockey fan. People tell me I'm being over-analytical. I mean, what defines a "true" hockey fan? Can't fans be wealthy? The answer is yes, they can. But don't tell me the sport of hockey hasn't drifted away from its grassroots core. A massive portion of dedicated NHL fans will never get to see a single game due to nothing other than money. Corporate greed has always been around, but today's ticket prices are fucking ridiculous. I know, I know, salaries are huge as well, and players have to take some blame. Whatever the case, the power of the almighty dollar and elimination of middle-class superfans has never defined the game more than it does now.

After a rough start, dealing with my nerves and inexperience, I had had a decent camp. As I said earlier, any young player with a love for the game respects the rich history of the Habs, and dealing with that pressure can be overwhelming at times. I definitely made some mistakes that September, but played okay in the rookie games and got my ass kicked by a few heavyweights, including longtime NHL enforcer Donald Brashear (I didn't think I was gonna beat these guys — I was just trying to show the brass how desperately I wanted to make the team), which left a few scars on my noggin but landed me a spot in the lineup for a few exhibition games and put a smile on my face that lasted well into November. I haven't seen many professional sporting exhibition matches, but in hockey the set-up is very similar to a regular season game, especially in Montreal and Toronto. Games are sold out, and most lineups feature the bulk of the team's stars — sprinkled with the odd rookie like me. Coaches look at potential trades and tweak the lineup for their opening day roster, and in my case the organization was giving me some experience to take back to junior and letting me feel more like a part of the Montreal Canadiens, my favourite NHL franchise since I was a toddler.

My first exhibition game could be a chapter in itself (the hardest thing about writing this book is narrowing down the stories), but let's just say things went well. Jacques Demers put me on the first line with Mark Recchi (Rex) and Pierre Turgeon—as he had in some of the intra-squad games—and I was so nervous I remember very little about the game itself and an awful lot about the cameras, media, fans, and celebrities whichever way I turned. I was sweaty and jumpy, with emotions flying at me from all directions. It was such an indescribable moment for an 18-year-old superfan—and I actually felt claustrophobic. Once the game started, I literally had to close my eyes and compose myself—I had started to hyperventilate and shed tears of joy before my first shift.

When the left winger on the line before me, Pierre Sevigny, came to the bench at the end of his shift, I leaped onto the ice with more pride than I had ever known—and I felt so very free. I felt at home, with a sense of accomplishment that made the Entry Draft pale in comparison. I was playing for the Montreal Canadiens. I was living one of my dreams, so it all seemed strangely familiar. It was also the first time I'd ever played in a real game without a visor. The wind in my face and the freedom I felt playing a game with the best adults on the planet was a metaphor for the freedom I felt as an 18-year-old boy. In many ways, it represented my real introduction to manhood—the intensity of the situation, the fact that my dream was coming true, changed me forever. The long, hard road I had taken—filled with mental and physical adversity that will only ever really be known to my family and myself—finally showed signs of paying off. I remember becoming more confident every time I had the puck, thinking, *This is the* NHL *and I just made a good pass . . . maybe I can play in this league.*

Mark—Rex—was awesome. He calmed me down and pointed out that I had better junior numbers than most people on the ice. They were just a little older and more experienced, he explained. As luck would have it, I scored a goal that game and had a great tilt—a toe-to-toe battle with the 32-year-old Steve Leach. By game's end, I was happy with my effort. The goal was lucky—Rex had thrown the biscuit out of the corner and it bounced off my leg and into the cage—but hey, it was still a goal.

Mr. Demers liked what he saw and asked me if I wanted to play the next night—in Maple Leaf Gardens. I immediately called my buds back on the Rock and told them to bring a pile of bodies to Green Sleeves in downtown St. John's the next night. I was going to play, on live television, against the Toronto Maple Leafs.

My promise to fight Domi had completely slipped my mind, but Blair made sure I remembered early the next morning, calling my room at the Chateau Champlain hotel in Montreal to make sure he caught me before we departed for T-Dot. I'd felt pressure the night before—but this was different. The guys at least knew I was an okay player after the first game, and I needed to earn that respect, but I would also show them I wasn't afraid of anything. With first-game jitters behind me, I was almost anxious to get back out there.

I don't consider myself a "tough guy," but one of the things I like about hockey is the fact that sometimes you can win just by showing up to the battle. This isn't the case in most sports played throughout history. In ancient Rome a gladiator would literally be killed if he just "showed up"—winning was that important. The same goes for all the battles and wars that have ever been fought. Boxing, ultimate fighting, karate . . . I can keep going, but most sports or social situations that allow fighting don't leave much room for the spirited participant who doesn't win. Hockey is beautiful that way. You need talent and a high degree of finesse to play, but a major part of the game is standing up for yourself and your teammates in different situations, and getting to know those situations makes for a good leader. I try not to overuse the word "warrior" like some people do — after all, it's just a game — but players who have a warrior-like spirit stand to have a great degree of success in the hockey world. I could cite numerous examples, but just look at Dustin Brown during the L.A. Kings' Cup run in 2012. He took his team into battle, leading by example, and that was how I was taught to play the game too, by men like my father; my minor hockey coach, Derm Connolly; and my junior coaches, Bob Loucks and Rick Carriere.

Anyway, as I was in a taxicab on the way to the Gardens before the game I decided I really was going to fight Tie. I was reading an issue of *Rolling Stone* and my promise was hovering in the back of my mind, so I threw the mag down and said, "Fuck it, I'm fightin' him." I had nothing to lose, I thought, and could only earn respect. Nobody in the building expected me to win a fight against Tie Domi, so there was no pressure from that perspective. He was one of the toughest men in the league (arguably one of the toughest ever) and at the time had had tilts with Probie that are now called legendary. Tie was short but had a great centre of gravity and would rely on that heavily during his illustrious career as an enforcer, along with the fact he was a lefty, had a large, hard head, and had a knack for fighting. He was genuinely good at it — and don't kid yourself, there's an art to hockey fighting.

On the way into the building there was a pay phone. It was actually right outside the dressing room. I stopped to call my pals — who were gathered at Green Sleeves in St. John's, a great pub now managed by my pals Stefan Hancock and Jody Temple, and the cornerstone of George Street — and told them to get a good seat, I was going to get this over with as early as possible. Blair was living in Toronto at that time and came to watch the game with two other high school pals, Jason Foote and Greg Dunne. I saw them during warm-up and we all had a good laugh, me on one side of the glass skating with the Montreal Canadiens, and them eating popcorn and reading the program!

During warm-up, it's typical for players to stretch in a stationary position, and this usually means close to the red line, which splits the rink into two even zones. Guys who have experience tend to hang out by the line and shoot the shit before the game. When I saw Tie stretch, I glided over his way and got down on one knee. "Mr. Domi, can I have a word?" I said politely, in an autograph-seeker's tone.

"Sure, kid, fire away," replied Tie, who was now looking into my eyes, curious and attentive.

"Well, I was, kinda . . . uh . . . wondering . . . if . . . you wanna fight tonight, er, maybe?"

"Well, not really; but it sometimes works out that way," he said with a chuckle, obviously confusing my invitation with childlike curiosity. "Who wants to go? Stevenson? Rivet? It's exhibition, kid, but if I have a reason I'll fight, of course. It comes with the territory."

"Well, no, I wasn't referring to them, sir. I was referring to, well, me."

Tie stopped stretching and glared intimidatingly for three or four seconds before smiling and saying, "Fuck, they get younger every year! I'm not fighting you kid, but I respect the balls . . ."

Back then I was surprised Domi knew how old I was; but now that I am older I am not surprised at all. Players in the NHL are there for a reason, and Tie Domi's success was no fluke. He studied lineups to see who might be the next young up-and-coming enforcer wanting to take away his title. He did his homework and, to varying degrees, knew who every player on our roster was. I was far from a tough guy—nothing at all for him to be worried about—just a rookie who wanted some respect, but I had penalty minutes comparable to many heavyweights, which puts you on the tough guys' radars. Sometimes you just have to be willing to take a beating to gain more room and respect on the ice, and I figured this was as good a time as any. Outside of being a team game, it's your livelihood, and one roster spot can make a difference of millions of dollars, so I wanted to earn that respect as quickly as possible. Team becomes family in that sense, and everyone wants what's best for their family.

After returning to the dressing room for the 20-minute break before the game started, I told a few of the boys about my conversation with Domi. I distinctly remember Craig Rivet's enthusiastic laugh, and the next thing I knew the game was about to start. As I listened to legendary Maple Leafs public address announcer Paul Morris read the starting lineups, I looked over at Blair on the other side of the glass and winked. As one of my best friends, he knew I was crazy enough to do what it took to make good on my promise.

The game started, and after nine long minutes thinking I was never going to get a shift anytime soon, my name was called and I leapt over the boards. It was just like that first time in Montreal—except my skate got caught on the boards during the jump and I fell more awkwardly than a rhinoceros on a slip-and-slide in the rain. I landed on my face. If only I was wearing a visor . . .

The whistle blew and I noticed Tie. One of the Leafs pushed one of our players and I beelined towards the pack, knowing Domi was following behind me like a shark circling his prey.

Fuckin' right! I was going to get my wish! Although, with a sober second thought, I wanted to abort mission as soon as I could. What the fuck was I thinking? Tangle with Tie Domi? Another stupid promise. Fuck. I was drunk with self-importance after a good game in Montreal, and now I was going to pay for it—taught a lesson by a physically superior member of our species and one of hockey's all-time legends.

I could sense the man's presence; he was getting closer and closer . . . And then all of a sudden I was at centre ice in Maple Leaf Gardens, in a televised NHL game, fighting Tie Domi.

It was awesome.

Tie spun me around and as we struggled for positioning he let me get set—and then he started to beat my cocky, zit-filled adolescent face hard with his weathered fists. I was scrambling like a non-swimmer in the deep end, gasping for air and swinging randomly, but once in awhile I'd feel my fist hit him even though I had my eyes closed, so I knew I was doing better than expected just by getting a single punch in. I actually fell down at the start of our dust-up and Tie stopped clobbering me long enough for me to get back up. I then proceeded to take a shit-kickin' from a legend. I resembled Bambi on that ice, but it remains one of my greatest hockey memories. At the end of the tilt I went down hard after taking another Tie Domi left and felt some blood trickle down my lip.

Even more awesome!

When we got to the penalty box, Tie was a class act. He thanked me for the tilt and complimented my character, and for the remainder of our five-minute sin-bin stay we chatted, understanding the fact that underneath the show there was a level of humanity about the whole thing. We were both just hockey players, doing our job.

After that night in September '95, I fought Tie two more times (1996 and 1997) but never came close to recapturing that first adrenaline rush. Sometimes you have to live for the moment, and I think sometimes being impulsive can be a good thing. I never got the chance at a long NHL career, but I took advantage of the time I had.

I saw Tie again a few years ago, in a pub in Halifax. I wasn't sure if he would remember me so I kept to myself, hanging on the opposite side of the place with a few of my buddies: Chad "Snakes" Graham,

Steve "Billy" Halfyard and Steve "Spock" Kelly. As we sipped our beer and ate hot wings, I told the boys the story I've just mentioned here, to a series of laughs. Eventually, Tie came over, winked, and said "Cheers, kid," patting me on the back before walking out the door. Right then, the waitress told me and my pals he had paid our tab.

Thanks, Tie.

And folks: that's hockey.

Rewf

The first day of my first NHL camp was nerve-racking. As the most recent first-rounder, I felt some stress, which was normal. I was the highest-picked player to audition for Les Habitants since Shayne Corson, almost a decade before me. There was more pressure on me than a female elephant during mating season. But seriously, expectations were high. And then there was the unreal feeling of pride and honour: I was a Montreal Canadien; it's something I wouldn't trade for the world, and something most hockey players never get to experience.

I was in awe just walking around the streets of Montreal, being part of the everyday buzz of a city so rich in culture and history. The language was new for me—that up close and personal, at least. The restaurants were exquisite and plentiful. An artistic flavour permeated the city as buskers played their instruments on the street corners and artists created paintings at the drop of a dime. And the women. Oh my goodness, the women! The threes dressed like nines, and the rest made you want to undergo a complete makeover before even thinking about making a pass. The girls all looked like they'd jumped off magazine covers — the everyday women were from *Vogue*; the businesswomen from *Playboy*; the strippers came from *Penthouse*.

I was 18 . . . enough said.

And then it was off to the hockey rink — like most other days of my life, except in this case the rink was the Montreal Forum. One of the most storied buildings in all of professional sports, it was Canada's answer to Yankee Stadium.

Outside the Forum there were a couple of dozen fans waiting to get autographs before practice. It was new to me, but I quickly came to realize that in Montreal it was like this before every practice or game. It helped to push my anxiety over the top, and I felt as if it was a dream. I had been nervous before, but nothing like this — I was mesmerized by the sheer joy not only of knowing I was in the building that housed so many legends but realizing I was about to become a part of their tradition.

The first hour I spent at the Forum that day is still vivid in my mind, and I remember gulping while meeting guys like Lyle Odelein, Mike Keane, Mark Lamb, and Patrick Roy. The thing is, in the home city of Les Habitants, meeting the players for the first time takes a back seat, in terms of awe-inspired wonder, to actually being in the historic Forum. I felt like a student of ancient Rome visiting the Colosseum for the first time. The media were around every corner, looking to catch any new Habs gossip, stuff that wouldn't qualify as page-filler anywhere else on planet earth. I wept uncontrollably in the bathroom stall before we hit the ice, hoping nobody would see me, and had the butterflies so bad I puked. This wasn't entirely a bad thing. Now I had a reason as to why my eyes were tearing up! I wish someone had snapped my picture. The look on my face must have been comical.

That day we were having a practice, and a red versus white intra-squad game was to follow shortly after. I noticed halfway through warm-up that a lineup for our game was posted behind the bench, so I scooted over to glance at my linemates for the day. I had a little hop in my step by that point, and at least a few nerves had smartened up and listened to my many prayers to calm down. A few seconds later, that thought was squashed when I saw who was on my line for camp: Pierre Turgeon and Mark Recchi — seasoned vets with an abundance of talent and possible future Hall of Fame candidates. I began sweating like Roger Clemens on trial.

It wasn't long before Mark Recchi himself skated over and apologized for not introducing himself in the dressing room. I told him I wouldn't hold it against him, and I went to lean on the boards but didn't notice the door was open. I fell. Wedged halfway between the bench and the ice, on my back, I looked up at Mark Recchi with tears still drying in the corners of my eye and a little vomit on my bottom lip for good measure. I was fucked. How could things get any worse?

As I tried gaining my composure, the invisible walls started to cave in on me and I couldn't stop stuttering. Cosmo Kramer would have been smoother trying to get up, and after what seemed like an eternity (but was only 15 or 20 seconds) I was back on my feet. Even for a rookie I was obviously shaken. I was breathing like I had taken an extra-long shift in a playoff game, and I was standing perfectly still. In a word, I looked ridiculous.

Mark laughed and said, "I am Mark Recchi, but you can call me Rex." I was like a four-year-old meeting Spider-Man — and now I was supposed to play on a line with the guy. As I looked at him, hyper-aware of my awkwardness, my mind raced a mile a minute. I wondered how to introduce myself. Of course, "Terry" was the appropriate, even normal answer. And it should have rolled off my tongue. But in a millisecond I changed my mind and figured I'd throw out my nickname as well. I meant to spit out "Newf," but I guess I was panting too hard, and on the verge of hyperventilation, I said "Rewf." I mixed "Ryan" and "Newf" into one fantastic happy little word jumble that made no sense . . . or did it? The only way out of this mess as I saw it was to go with the flow and not correct myself. If nobody caught on, Rex would think "Rewf" was my nickname and would soon forget about it before it caught on.

Well, wouldn't you know it, during the game Turgeon hit Rex with a saucer pass that Jean Beliveau would have been proud of, and Recchi was stopped on a breakaway . . . with yours truly trailing the play and shoving the rebound "upstairs where Daddy keeps the porn mags." I just batted at the puck as it lay in the crease and it went in the highest part of the net, right under the crossbar; otherwise known as "roofing" the puck.

When we got to the bench, Rex sat next to me and said, "Wow, nice shot. Now I know why they call you Roof." The bad news? I was stuck with that nickname for camp (it phased itself out over time, and finally the next season I told the story in the dressing room during my first game, to an abundance of laughter).

Montreal Memories

You know, I really did love a lot of things about playing in Montreal. I enjoyed my time there, even though I didn't play that much. I'm really not complaining—this isn't going to be a sour grapes book. When it comes down to it, in 1999 I was the one who held out from camp, determined to get traded. And then later that season the Habs wound up having a record number of injuries. My buddy Arron Asham got his big break as a result, and also because of all his hard work, of course—he's a great hockey player who can do it all: fight, hit, and score. I played that style of game too. So, if nothing else, I probably would have been given a chance that year. Honestly, I harbour no grudge against the Canadiens organization and feel honoured to have worn the uniform. Back then I wanted to be an offensive contributor and believed I could be, but my passion for the game, combined with my stubborn, impulsive nature, clouded my vision. I was too anxious; I could be my own worst enemy that way. I complained about some guys having one-way contracts—but in reality it's hard to send those guys to the minors when you're paying them over a million bucks. We were in Fredericton, a.k.a. "Freddy Beach," making less than $100,000—so the team saved money by having prospects like myself, Brad Brown, Tomas Vokoun, or Craig Conroy suit up in the AHL. The thing I realize now is that's just hockey, the way it works. And yes, young players gain much-needed experience in the minors, so time spent in the AHL can be very rewarding.

As a first-rounder, I wanted to impress the city of Montreal and Habs Nation right away. The pressure to perform is immense, especially for a teenager. All those years of history; all that glory; all the legends who wore one of the sporting world's most famous uniforms, representing the winningest professional athletic franchise on the planet. I wanted to play regularly so I could carry the load for the fans and players of my generation. It sounds crazy, but at the core of my thoughts there was always a desire to bring a Stanley Cup to the NHL team I'd loved since childhood. It was disappointing, how it all ended up goin' down . . .

Now, was part of it an ego thing? Hell yeah. When they picked me in the top 10, I knew I could be the warrior who could lead the rest of the soldiers to war, and I knew we could win that war because I trusted the management to provide our army with the tools to get the job done. I am sure the subconscious understanding that if I did deliver I would be loved for it was also attractive to my ego. The NHL, however, is a grind. And remember, there are 29 other teams . . . Winning is tough, and things like injuries and luck factor into the puzzle in a big way as well. The whole time I was part of the Habs organization, we all felt we had the parts to win someday sooner than later.

Timing is huge, and I was a little anxious when it came to playing in the bigs. After junior ended and I entered pro, I was coached by Michel Therrien for two years in Fredericton as a member of the Habs farm team, the Fredericton Canadiens. After my rookie-of-the-year season in Fredericton in 1997–98 (21 goals, 39 points, 256 PIMs), I thought I would be on the big team for sure. I had over 30 fighting majors and over 20 goals. However, I spent all of 1998–99 in Freddy as well — even though I played fewer games, had more points, and regularly fought heavyweights, usually to respectable outcomes. At the end of the year I was pissed off and I decided I wanted to be traded to another organization, for a fresh start if nothing else. At this point, when I was called up to play with Montreal I was fighting pretty much every shift. I'm not blaming anyone for that — I wanted to get involved in the game, and if I wasn't on the ice much, I'd try to mix it up a bit, partly due to my impulsive nature. I was gonna get on that score sheet somehow, and if that meant fighting a willing combatant like Todd Harvey or Cam Russell (two players I really looked up to), so be it. I had no fear as far as taking a punch to the face, so I figured this was an attribute that would separate me from other players trying to win a job on the big club. I still think it did, and I still think I would have been a good player up there, but I am aware I went about it the wrong way.

I wish I could see all the guys again now — I don't feel the older guys on the Habs of the late 1990s really knew me that well. I was a nervous kid, trying to fit in. I never really just sat back and acted like, well, me. Most of the boys were great to me: Turner Stevenson, Brian Savage, Mark Recchi, Stephane Quintal, Shayne Corson, Craig Rivet, Vinnie Damphousse, Scott Thornton, Stephane Richer . . . these are just a handful of the guys who really made us younger players feel comfortable on and off the ice. I know I mention a lot of people here, but I don't want to leave anyone out, they were all so important in shaping me as a person. Now that I look back, I have an even deeper appreciation, because they really went out of their way to include us and make us feel accepted. That kind of thing eases a guy's nerves and makes life a lot less complicated in a situation that can be very stressful.

I always admired Turner Stevenson because he had so much heart and determination. He was probably the worst skater I have seen at that level, but he got the job done. He was unorthodox, but that almost gave him an edge. He was a much smarter player than people gave him credit for, and he had great timing as far as hits and fights go, lifting the team when the situation called for it. His skill was deceptive because of his style. He was also good at balancing out a dressing room and making sure everyone was on the same page before we hit the ice. Turner wasn't my best buddy or anything—we hardly spoke sometimes—but when I saw him hoist the Stanley Cup in '03 as a member of the New Jersey Devils, I broke out a six-pack and got a buzz on for him. He'll make a good coach, because he is living proof that hard work and a good attitude pay off.

Some of the crazy shit I would do to keep the boys loose was ridiculous. I wanted to be accepted immediately—I was always onstage. This can work for you or against you, of course, so if you're gonna fuck around you better make sure you don't go too far and piss people off. Once when we were on the west coast and Gwen Stefani was in the hotel lobby, I asked her what she'd like me to do to spread some good vibes throughout the room, as we had been waiting over an hour for our rooms after a mix-up at the front desk. No Doubt were a huge band at the time, so just getting the chance to meet her was a thrill. She said we should all relax and go for a swim while we waited — the hotel we were staying at apparently had a five-star pool area. Before anyone could say "spiderwebs," I leapt into the colossal fountain in the lobby — wearing my brand new Hugo Boss three-piece suit — and swam laps for the entertainment of everyone in attendance, gaining the attention of the security guards in the process. The guards were laughing but reprimanded me pretty hard. They helped me out of the water as I threw the suit in the garbage and headed towards the hotel bar in waterlogged underwear and my drenched dress shoes (apparently it was okay for a half-naked 19-year-old — 21 was legal drinking age — to wet his whistle with a rum and coke in the piano bar, but swimming in the fountain would not be tolerated), signing autographs like I was the captain of the team.

Trading Places

My best buddy growing up was Jeremy "Taz" Charles — I mentioned him in the first part of this book. When we were 19, I was playing for the Habs and he was living on the Rock, having recently returned from giving junior hockey a shot in Port Colborne, Ontario. Jeremy had decided that lifestyle wasn't for him and entered business school at Memorial University. Like so many other kids, he dropped out after realizing he had no idea what he wanted to do with his life. Taz needed a change, and I was happy he made the move to Montreal shortly afterwards with his beautiful future wife, Sarah Parker. Jeremy started working at Le Château on Saint Catherine Street in downtown Montreal, near the Molson Centre, but quickly realized his heart was in the foods industry. He enrolled in culinary school and finally had a goal I believed he could attain. I enjoyed having my best pal with me in the big city, because after all, we were teenagers on the brink of becoming adults. In Montreal the process was accelerated, and this was all new to us.

I can't remember exactly when, but at some point during the season, my teammate and chum Shayne Corson offered Jeremy a job working in the kitchen of his newly opened restaurant downtown. Jeremy and I would accompany Shayne and Darcy Tucker to dinner frequently, and the job offer came up over some red wine one night. Cors introduced me to virtually everything I know about dining out, and always made sure to invite the young fellas when he hit the town. I really enjoy those memories — Shayne was a good guy and teammate.

When Jeremy began working at Shayne's, I would pop in daily for a pint or an appetizer, and I'd usually have a chat with the house bartender, a fellow by the name of Sam Roberts. Sam was an aspiring musician and a decent hockey player. As I said, Jeremy was a good player too; he skated like the wind and went all-out all the time, like the Tasmanian Devil; hence the nickname. He had been scouted to play in Ontario as a 16-year-old but got homesick. The three of us hung out quite a bit, often playing a game of pick-up hockey and having a few beers afterwards. I enjoyed Sam's company and many times my two free game tickets (every player gets a pair) would be given to Sam and Jeremy.

As time progressed and Jeremy and Sam gained experience, they quickly accelerated to the top of their fields. I'll be the first to admit the boys worked hard, and I would have bet they'd be successful in their respective industries, but I wasn't prepared for what the future would soon hold for these two great young lads. I don't think anyone saw it coming!

Jeremy, to make a long story short, has become a world-renowned chef in the last decade or so. After making a name for himself in Montreal, Jeremy moved on to bigger and better things in Chicago, working in the industry for half a decade and gaining valuable experience in the process. He had a vision. When he and Sarah got married in Newfoundland a half-dozen years ago, Jeremy set his eyes on opening his own restaurant back in his home province, and I'm happy to say he is currently "living the dream," as they say in the business. Jeremy first worked at Atlantica — a great five-star restaurant in Portugal Cove, Newfoundland, with great food and a breathtaking view — and after much success (Atlantica would become one of Canada's "Best New Restaurants" in 2007, according to *enRoute* magazine) he finally saw his dream come to fruition when Raymonds opened in downtown St. John's in 2011. *enRoute* voted it the number one new restaurant in the country. Over the course of his professional journey, Jeremy has also received many personal accolades for his efforts.

Sam, meanwhile, has literally become a rock star. He exploded onto the Canadian music scene with the release of the EP *The Inhuman Condition* in 2002, which featured mega-hits "Brother Down" and "Don't Walk Away Eileen," and has released many fine albums since. I really dig his music. Sam is a family man and remains grounded. When he comes to town, I often see him over a beer or some fish and chips. In 2003, Sam performed at the Molson Canadian Rocks for Toronto concert, better known as the SARS benefit concert. He was chosen, along with acts like AC/DC, Blue Rodeo, and Justin Timberlake, to open for the Rolling Stones in front of half a million people on a beauty day in late June. I had goosebumps during his entire performance and still laugh every time I think of Sammy slingin' me rum-and-cokes just a few years previous.

Sam and I both attended Jeremy's wedding, which was right

before he moved home and achieved Canadian notoriety, but he had been working privately for some big-time players in North America at that point and was becoming a name within the industry. I stood for him, and for my speech I wrote a poem. Jeremy actually found this for me at his house, so I figured I'd put it in here for all to read! Here it is:

I met Jeremy Charles back in '83
But I knew him before he knew me,
No one could see where he was comin' from,
I mean the dude stood out like a very sore thumb

We were all kids with fun-lovin' dreams
And he's in the corner with GQ magazine
Even at hockey, under his gear,
He'd be wearin' his Hugo Boss underwear
A good guy, mind you, always in a good mood,
But was overly interested in fashion and food

We became pals and hung out every day,
In spite of the fact everyone thought he was gay
As time went on and we entered our teens,
He talked about women and his weird, erotic dreams
Don't get me wrong, we played lots of sports too,
Hockey, baseball, and soccer, just to name a few

Jeremy was a friend on whom I could always rely
So when he'd swipe my hockey cards I'd turn a blind eye

We argued and fist-fought like any normal kids,
But I did more damage than he ever did,

If I was mad about anything—girls or a test,
I'd give him a beating on his arms, neck, and chest,
Taz, as we called him, would put up a good fight,
And I'd have a few bruises by the end of the night,

Most of the time, though, there was no harm done,
And we always made sure to keep having fun,

Then came the time I had to move away,
With a good hockey offer, I just had to go play
We were both pretty shaken that late August night,
I was leavin' the next day on a six-thirty flight
As we slept side by side I thought as I lay,
"He's not makin' a move, he's definitely not gay,"

Time then moved on but we both kept in touch,
All that really changed was I didn't get home much
Jeremy stayed loyal, a really good lad,
Even calling to say congrats after my high school grad

Then I was drafted to the Habs—in the top ten!
And so in Montreal we were united again
He was right in his element and felt like a pro,
Drinkin' red wine, workin' at Le Château
He had friends in high places—free tickets to Habs games,
There started to be a buzz at the mention of his name

Hangin' with Shayne in his brand new wheels,
Smokin' fat cigars, eatin' expensive meals
He was livin' the life and was nobody's fool

He even tricked Sam Roberts into thinkin' he was cool

And when I met Sarah? My hat was off to the cat,
How'd a nerd like this get a girl like that?

She was beautiful and friendly so the joke was on me
I was single and soon out-of-hock-ey

They both stayed in love, nothing got in the way
As evidenced by the fact they got married today

To both of you, congrats, from the bottom of my heart,
I hope that from here on, you're never apart

Thanks Sarah for making Jeremy so very content
I can't explain how much our friendship has meant

And Taz, I'm a friend, but without a doubt
If you ever get divorced, I'm askin' her out!

TR 2006

It's funny. At one point, I was in the NHL, at the top of my field, and I was giving my free tickets to a couple of guys who worked in a restaurant, low on the totem pole so to speak. Within a few years, Jeremy had become a fantastic chef who is still gaining momentum and is known globally, and Sammy ended up opening for the Rolling Stones and becoming a rock star in his own right. By then I was playing senior hockey for the Mount Pearl Blades and working as a sales rep for Red Bull Energy Drink. Oh, how life can be a roller coaster ride! I'm laughing as I write this. It's rich. But man, I am proud of the boys. Such humble beginnings, such focus, such success . . . and such good friends.

Barbie & Ken

Me and some of the boys were at a strip club in Detroit called BT's. It was the night before Halloween in Motown: Devil's Night. Now, I wasn't completely familiar with all that this entails, but I knew it meant a night of mischief that sometimes resulted in violence. Apparently its origins were in Michigan (this is what I heard but it could be a total falsehood—it adds to the story, though). All the strippers were in costume that evening, and one of the cougars, dressed as everyone's favourite blond doll, came over and introduced herself as "Barbie." I told her that my name was Ken and that we were a natural couple. She was 40 or older and at the end of her shift. We made small talk long enough for her to tell me her favourite player was Stevie Y, and within five minutes I was in this chick's car en route to her trailer for an evening of bangin' with no strings attached. I was pretty excited about it, to be honest.

When we got to her place, however, I became a little apprehensive. We'd passed our fair share of fire trucks, ambulances, and police cars, and there were even cop cars parked across the street from her trailer, cherries lit up with the occasional siren-chime to keep some order to whatever ugly situation had taken place over there. When we got inside her door, she called some dude named "Skull" who showed up before I had my second shoe off. He dropped her off some GHB (a drug she said made her horny for young stallions like me), which she promptly downed. She told me to relax; she had to shower and would be right back. I was turned on and tuned in myself, obviously, but also a little worried that I wouldn't make it back in time for our 7 a.m. bus to the airport; I had no clue where I was, and it was already 1:30. This broad wasn't going anywhere, and the neighbourhood I was in didn't really seem all that taxicab-friendly. Fuck it, though; I'd worry about that when the time came. We all know hormones can make a guy do crazy things, especially a single 19-year-old making decent money playing a professional sport. It's all about balancing the line between access and excess. I took her advice, relaxed as much as I could, and waited for my stripper date to return so I could get my oil changed and split.

Five minutes later, Barbie came into the room with a plan. She was dressed in black latex and told me to sit the fuck down and listen to Momma. She bent me over, shoved a thin yellow dildo up my rear end, and slapped me across the face, calling me her hockey bitch! I was fuckin' terrified, to be honest, but I went along with it for one full spin of Metallica's "The Unforgiven," which was playing in the background. I couldn't handle the banana-like obstruction in my ass, so I took it out, reached for a whip off her wall and flipped her around. I spread her legs, took out my tool and "sank the Bismarck." I proceeded to whip her bottom and pound away while she writhed in non-stop ecstasy with the aid of the love drug she'd ingested. I was the king.

When we were done, I high-fived my stripper pal as she lay comfortably content in a pile of various bodily fluids, and told her I had to bolt. She understood, and I got Skull to give me a lift to my hotel, which was around a 20-minute trek. He was happy to do so, as long as I signed a few hockey cards and gave him 100 bones. This was fine by me. When he dropped me off, the sun was about to come up, and I knew I might be in the doghouse if anyone knew where I had been. We had the day off — it was a travel day — and were headed to San Jose to start a western swing, so I wasn't fucked up for practice or anything, but at the same time I was 19 and getting back way too late (I had my cell on me, though, and I knew there were a couple other guys who'd gone out and got lucky as well).

I went right to Mario Tremblay, the coach at the time, and confessed. I told him the story from start to finish, and after he relayed the message to the other coach on hand that morning (Steve Shutt, I believe) they let me off pretty easy, in hindsight, although I was upset at the time. They fined me $250, made me tell the story at the front of the bus on the way to the airport, and skated me extra hard after practice for a week. I fuckin' deserved it, though. When I was sent back to junior later that year I told my buddies in Red Deer, and they were speechless. That's a helluva thing to happen to a teenager!

On the Juice, With the Juice

1997–98 was a fun year for me, and for most of the Fredericton Canadiens. The club had been Montreal's farm team for the better part of a decade, but for the '97–98 season we were the combined minor-league affiliate of the Habs and the Los Angeles Kings. There were 9 or 10 Kings hopefuls — including Roman Vopat, Chris Schmidt, Donald "Daddy Mac" MacLean, Eric Belanger, and Josh "Juice" Green — playing with a slew of young Montreal prospects, including yours truly, Jose Theodore, David Ling, Brad Brown, Tomas Vokoun, and Stephane Robidas.

We were all in our early 20s and having the time of our lives. Most of us were entering our first full pro season, and that meant going through a lot in the short few summer months after junior. All of a sudden, the paycheques were huge (I made $120 a week as a

19-year-old in Red Deer and close to $2,000 a week in Freddy Beach). In junior we lived with a roommate and billets; now we were free to live on our own. Travel had become easier too; roadside motels were replaced by four-star hotels. Everyone was of legal drinking age, so, after games, cards and beer became the norm. The high school girls of junior morphed into a wide variety of women ready to get physical with future has-beens for no other reason than their kids had our hockey cards. The cities were a step up—and players were suddenly required to have nice suits to wear to each game, not just an old white shirt with a cheap tie and jacket. Beers and chewing tobacco took a back seat to Scotch and cigars after some games. Like David Wilcox says in one of his many beloved classic tunes, "Downtown Came Uptown." On top of all this, at some point during that season most of us got called up to the Big Show, where four stars become five, Scotch becomes Cristal, the Aitken Centre becomes the Bell Centre, and the women are stacked.

Our typical day meant being at the rink by 8 or 9 and practising between 10 and 12. Then maybe there'd be a workout. After that? It's all free time for the most part, and would often include restaurants, pubs, taverns, bars, clubs, patios, and lounges. We picked our spots to tie one on, but if you have ever seen the movie *Slap Shot*, I'd have to say it's a fairly accurate portrayal of the minor leagues. Even if we weren't boozing, we were hangin' out, and being in a smaller town like Freddy Beach brought us even closer together. We bonded like brothers in many local dives.

Whenever we got to the rink in the morning, there was usually a good story from the night before. Oftentimes, a player might be sent down from the NHL and have some Big Show stories to share over stale coffee and whatever doughnuts were brought in that day by the rookies. It was something to look forward to on cold winter mornings, and it only added to the camaraderie that keeps a young kid on track. A lot of fans don't realize how stressful pro hockey can be. Even though we do what we love, there are sacrifices and pressures that are hard to deal with. A scoring slump can end in demotion, while a few good games can be rewarded with a call-up to Montreal or L.A. It really is that simple at times — and a few points or penalty minutes can be the difference between thousands, hell, millions of bucks. Let's just say it can generate a high level of stress for a kid.

Anyway, on this one particular day, Roman Vopat, who had just been demoted by the Kings, was telling us a great story about a day off for the team in L.A. a few days earlier. One of the Kings veterans bet Roman he couldn't drink 24 beers in 8 hours. Vopes said he tried, but it was way harder than it looked.

"That sounds easy, eight hours is child's play, Vopes!" I said.

"I know you think so, but it's not," said Roman — a good guy, tough player, and chick magnet who hailed from the Czech Republic but played his junior in the Western Hockey League. He was always up for a good time or a challenge. "There are rules," he said. "There can be no eating and no puking. The beer has to be full bodied — none of this light shit. There will be no consumption of water during the time allotted, and we all have to witness you attempt this feat."

"Perfect," I rebutted. "I'll smash that time, and quite frankly, Roman, I am offended you don't think I can do it. I am also flabbergasted that a man of your so-called experience and pride couldn't pull it off. We're on, brutha."

I believe the over/under was set at 18 beers, and more than a few guys took a part of the action. It happened to be St. Paddy's Day, and we had the following morning off, so as a collective group of idiots we all headed to Dolan's Pub after practice to hang out at the table next to the women's washroom. We did this in order to make sure we got a glance at every dame in the place who might possibly end up with her clothes in our laundry the next morning . . .

I sat down with Matt Higgins, Boyd Olson, Juice, Chris Schmidt, and my roomie, Miloslav Guren. Most of the team was there, but I distinctly remember sitting down with those guys and ordering my first Guinness. I remember because Juice pointed out I should be going with a bottle instead of a pint, as I was now drinking more than was required, and it could play a part in the outcome. I told him to relax; his coin was safer than *Titanic*'s box office record.

"Juice," I said, smirking, "this is a walk in the park. Don't sweat it. Happy St. Paddy's Day, *mes amis*. Cheers!" With that we all touched glasses and sat back to take in the vibrant atmosphere of one of Freddy Beach's coolest poison providers.

Things were looking good early. A few of the boys were junior rivals (Schmidt — Seattle; Juice — Swift Current; Higgins — Moose Jaw), and Boyd and I were telling them how I used to turn the heat on full blast in their dressing rooms when they came to play in Tri-Cities so they'd be exhausted on the ice. We all took turns leading the conversation, and we actually made a side bet that I couldn't make it to 10 beers without a trip to the men's room. I broke the seal at number 11, and therefore had already won free beer for the day. I do have to confess that around beer number four I switched to bottles. I figured Juice had a valid argument. It wasn't just my money I was gambling with, and I would drink more Guinness after the challenge if I wanted.

Time was passing and things were going as smoothly as Mario Lemieux on a breakaway in his heyday. It looked like I was in the clear. I hit beer number 20 in full stride, and although I had a slur and my shirt was off, I was still going strong. I looked like a fool, sure — but that's not the bet, now, is it? Just four more wobbly pops and I win. I looked at my watch when Juice pointed out the obvious:

we were only approaching the five-hour mark! I had over three hours to drink four more!

I immediately went after Roman to start celebrating. He was equally inebriated, and the female patron he was focusing on had the sex appeal of a plane crash. His beer goggles were thick and blurry.

"Roman, get your wallet out and let's have a shooter to celebrate." We had tequila, and I had four beers left. Easy as pie.

Next thing I knew I was stumbling around outside, stammering my way through Bruce Springsteen lyrics. Soon after this, Juice came out to look for me. He found me with my pants down and my hammer out, lying in a bank of yellow snow.

He threw me in a cab, he says. But I remember nothing.

The next morning, the phone rang for what seemed like hours. I woke wet—I swear, to this day it's the one and only time I pissed myself after hitting the sauce. The regurgitated pizza all over the floor suggested my pizza-eating dreams were not really dreams at all. The phone kept ringing. After about seven or eight calls, I finally answered. It was Earl Cronan, my roomie (in a Rhode Island accent): "TR, Mikey [Michel Therrien] called a practice. Me and Brownie slept at Higgy's last night so we took the cah and came straight to the rink. Mike said he phoned you first but there was no answa'. Congrats by the way, good job last night. That was a gutsy performance at the bah."

I was pissed. Mike and I didn't see eye to eye at the best of times, and I am pretty sure he called practice only because he'd heard about my antics the night before. When I got to the rink the boys stood up and clapped: the daily wager had clearly turned to whether or not I would make it to practice. The boys also filled me in on the night's events. I'd blacked out: it turns out I had finished 24 beers in a shade under five hours and 15 minutes.

Oh boy, you wanna talk sick? It was far and away the worst I have ever felt before hitting the ice. Nauseated, queasy, overheated, head pain . . . you name it, I felt it. I couldn't see straight. There was no preparation—we were supposed to have a day off! To add insult to injury, Mike made it a hitting practice—with no pucks—to prove a point. This ended up being a good thing for me because I wouldn't have been able to see the puck well enough to carry it down the ice, much less make a pass or take a shot. When he did bring pucks out they were given to D-men so a few of us forwards could practise . . . shot blocking! I fell asleep on the way home from practice in the passenger seat of Brownie's car and woke up five hours later in the driveway, cold as ice. What a day!

The Fisher King

The media can be hard to deal with, especially when you're not performing well, but I got along with most of the reporters and still keep in touch with many of the ones I've met. Usually members of the sports media are either ex-players or hardcore fans, so the setting is ripe for unique conversation and storytelling, which is right up my alley. I always thought about being a broadcaster/journalist after hockey because it keeps you in touch with the game on an intense level.

But this story is about one of the biggest letdowns of my life.

I always looked up to Red Fisher, the lead sports writer for the Montreal *Gazette*; he was respected everywhere in the world of sports and had covered the Montreal Canadiens since the mid-1950s. He knew many of the team's legends on a first-name basis and was, in my mind, a legend himself. A lifelong Habs fan, I couldn't wait to meet the guy. As a kid I mixed a love of hockey with a love of English, and had I not followed the yellow brick road to pro hockey I think I would have tried to pursue something related to books. I wanted to meet Red Fisher more than I wanted to meet Mark Recchi on my first day of camp. (Told ya I was a Habs fan!) When I was 13, I came face to face with him in the Forum but froze up, unable to speak! I never thought I would get the chance to meet him again.

As most people know, after practice in the bigs there's time for reporters to come in and shoot the shit with the players. They capture some footage and conduct the interviews that will become water-cooler talk the next day. I remember my first interview: it's something that isn't talked about often, but it really makes you feel like part of the squad. A reporter wants my input? Canada gives a shit what I have to say? Cool!

One particular day, when I was finally in the lineup for that evening's game, I was being interviewed by a couple of Montreal's finest — Herb Zurkowsky and Pat Hickey, I believe. I was in Montreal, in the Show, and on TV! I really felt like I was contributing to the team's legacy in some minute way.

Unfortunately Mr. Fisher didn't interview me, but that was fine. I didn't expect his attention; I figured I had to earn his respect first. Still, I was nervous, sweating. I took a swig of water, clenched my fists, smacked my hands together, and got myself psyched. I walked over to Mr. Fisher — who was standing in the corner, looking a little bored, loosely chatting with Mark Recchi as Rex checked out some new Hespeler twigs he had ordered — and stretched out my hand for him to shake. I was proud as a peacock. Mr. Fisher didn't hear me, so I did it again but now the nerves were kicking in. Again, no response. At this point it clicked . . . he couldn't hear me! He must have had a hearing aid. So I tapped him on the shoulder to make sure I was clear.

"It is an honour to meet you, Mr. Fisher!" I looked him in the eye and offered my hand for acceptance, hopefully beginning a new friendship.

No reply. What the fuck? The silence was so disturbing it was loud. Right then, my buddy Brad Brown called me over to chat.

"Red doesn't talk to rookies," Brownie said.

"Are you fuckin' kiddin' me?"

Brownie wasn't kidding at all; he was dead serious.

Red Fisher didn't talk to rookies. He didn't acknowledge you as a human being if you were a first-year player.

What kind of lame-ass bullshit was this? I mean, who is this guy, Frank fucking Sinatra? My opinion of this dude immediately plummeted. Currently I have more time for Perez fuckin' Hilton than Red Fisher. I mean, I have a high regard for experience and wisdom and all that, but if you can't treat me as a human being because of my place in a game that's supposed to be entertainment, then we have a problem. What's worse is that he made me feel nervous and intimidated. When you're a kid in the NHL, acceptance is important and confidence is crucial. The pressures and mental fatigue are enough. The last thing you need is some pig-headed writer becoming another obstacle.

A few years ago I was in Montreal, doing some work for the Team 990 radio station and noticed Red walking behind me, so I slowed and held open the door. Would you believe it, not even a thank-you? I proceeded to wish his wife well—she was sick at the time—and he still didn't acknowledge my existence.

And I fucking adored this ignorant man. I know I am gonna get a lot of flak for saying this, but it's like freeing myself of a monkey that's been on my back for far too long: Red, go fuck yourself. When I'm in my 70s and some 20-year-old wants to have a chat with me, man, I'm all ears.

I Am Canadien

The hardest part of accepting what became of my NHL career is that I will never really know if I was good enough to cut it in the Show. Not a day goes by that I'm not reminded of missed opportunities. Yes, I am confident in my abilities, but given my stats in other leagues against peers who became NHL stars, it's possible I would have been a decent NHLer, but I'll never be certain. Trying to make the Montreal Canadiens in the late '90s, many would say, was fighting an uphill battle. I don't know if I would go that far. It's a classy organization and they treated me well. I don't have a bad word to say about the vast majority of people I came across while part of the greatest franchise in hockey history. Even Rejean Houle and Alain Vigneault — the GM and coach of the team at the time I was in the minors — did okay by me. I thought Vigneault was a great coach, very respectful and on point. I thought they should have played me more, given me a better shot, but even in hindsight, that's just my opinion. They didn't think I was ready, and I respect that. I had some growing up to do, like most young kids with big junior stats. And if I'd never suffered what wound up being a career-ending injury in 2001, I think I would have made it back to the NHL because I am a very determined person. If I have one attribute that stood out on the ice, I think it would be determination.

There was one guy I didn't like at all, though: my American Hockey League coach from '97 to '99, Michel Therrien.

When the Habs drafted me, the GM was Serge Savard and the coach was Jacques Demers. They were great people and really seemed to like me (which goes without saying; they used their first pick in the '95 draft — the eighth overall — to select yours truly). I must admit, the organization didn't know much about me other than my stats, which seemed odd considering I had been interviewed by all but four teams leading up to the draft. Les Habitants were one of the few teams I hadn't had any contact with whatsoever. As my family and I made our way to the seating area on draft day morning in Edmonton, Montreal's head scout, Doug Robinson, congratulated me on a great season—mistaking me for Shane Doan. Nevertheless, the Canadiens chose me. They were always my favourite squad, so for me July 8, 1995, was and still is a day to celebrate (it is also my parents' wedding anniversary): I was a step closer to what I'd always felt was my true calling—playing and contributing for the Montreal Canadiens. I knew people back home on the Rock were partying big time now that I was the highest drafted player in the province's history. Back then, the Habs farm team was based out of Fredericton, so even if I went to the minors after junior I would be playing in my hometown against the St. John's Maple Leafs. The AHL Leafs were heroes to me too; I'd spent my teen years hoping that one day I could play hockey for a living just like them. One of their all-time legends, Todd Gillingham, was an idol of mine as a kid and is a close friend today.

After being drafted and being sent back to Tri-Cities, I was ready for my professional career to begin. I had two more years of junior left, and the anticipation was building every day. Around five games into the 1995–96 season, Jacques Demers got fired and the Habs brought in Mario Tremblay—a tough customer who'd won an incredible five Cups with Montreal as part of their 1970s dynasty. As I watched the news from Mark and Nancy Eby's house in Pasco, Washington, I was saddened that Mr. Demers was gone—he was a genuine guy who played a role in the decision to draft me. Worse, Serge Savard was also let go. The two gentlemen who had the most interest and influence on my future were no longer with the organization. Hiring Rejean Houle as GM was a curious decision. He'd won five championships with the team but was working for Molson at the time as a beer executive. He knew nothing about me. I'd felt protected with Demers and Savard around, and after all, if I fucked up it was their asses on the line for picking me in the first place. My agent, Mike Barnett, called me, however, and informed me of Tremblay's reputation as a character guy. I was aware of Tremblay's tenacious style on the ice, and I respected it.

During the Canadiens camp the following September, I went out of my way to impress Tremblay with my own tenacity. I scored some hard-nosed goals and volunteered for punching-bag duty against some of the league's heavyweights, most notably round two versus Tie Domi. I figured one thing I had control over was my level of intensity, and on the ice I was "gone mad," as they say on the Rock. As a result, I not only made the team as a 19-year-old, I was given Mario Tremblay's former jersey number, 14. This was great news and a sign that the organization had confidence in me. My mom and dad pointed out that most rookies entering the system of the storied Montreal franchise were assigned less common numbers, like 73 (Michael Ryder), 43 (Darcy Tucker), or 45 (Arron Asham).

To be honest, I really don't know how I made the squad: I played with post-concussion syndrome during camp. In January 1995, I had suffered a concussion with Tri-Cities in Seattle, and it actually took more than a year to heal. (Hall of Famer Pat LaFontaine called me every week, having been through the same situation, and made me feel comfortable in a very frustrating time. I appreciated that immensely. Great guy.) Luckily for me, the Habs had some injuries at the beginning of the season, and my junior club, the Americans, were projected to finish closer to the bottom than the top of the WHL standings. The Canadiens were forced into deciding to keep me around as a "black ace" (an extra guy on the roster who is used in the case of injuries or suspensions to other players). They figured I had accomplished a lot, statistically, in junior. Now they wanted me to improve my skills—things like passing, skating, and shooting. I guess they believed I could learn more from practising in the NHL than by playing in the WHL. I would eventually get sent back to junior in January—after the Red Deer Rebels made a trade for my rights—but not before playing my first four games in the big time. I was pumped, and I remember thinking it was a huge deal to have my own hockey card. I actually carried it around in my pocket! I still feel a giddy kind of a privilege about it—hockey cards are a classic part of childhood for a young hockey fan. A snippet of history.

From September until January that year, I actually lived with Darcy Tucker—an archrival of mine back in Tri-Cities who played for Kamloops and had one of the most successful junior hockey careers ever. The whole experience was surreal. One of Tuck's favourite meals at the time was Kraft Dinner and hot dogs; mine was pizza. I always had my PlayStation going; we played Crash Bandicoot for hours on end. There were movie posters on the walls and a basketball net on my door. We were just kids, but we'd recently become famous, rich, and historical. (This can be a lot to deal with, and I always say the best agents guide their clients through hockey's transitions, and that includes preparing to enter the league.) We drove my black 1996 Camaro around all winter like fools, and still couldn't believe we were in the NHL. I think our innocence was remarkable, given the situation.

This brings us to the 1997–98 hockey season, my first full year as a professional. Ninety percent of the time, a guy gets drafted and has a couple more years of junior ahead of him. The year you turn 20 is the year you typically enter the AHL. Of course, some guys play college hockey and some make the NHL at 18 or 19, but generally if you play major junior hockey, this is the path. I was fully aware of the fact that the four games I played with the Montreal Canadiens as a 19-year-old were a rare occurrence, and that in all likelihood I would be honing my talents in tropical Freddy Beach.

I was correct.

After a decent camp, I was given "the speech" by Mr. Houle — the one about working hard, acting professional, staying out of trouble and representing the Montreal Canadiens as best I could. It was early October, and I remember walking out of the Molson Centre towards the Chateau Champlain — one of Montreal's finest hotels and the site of much buffoonery amongst young campgoers and Hab hopefuls — wondering about the next phase of my unique journey.

In Freddy Beach, our coach was Michel Therrien. Mike had quite the reputation as a winner. In his short junior coaching career, he'd lost twice in the Quebec Major Junior Hockey League finals as head coach of the Laval Titan, and won the Memorial Cup championship in 1995–96 as head coach of the Granby Predateurs, bringing the QMJHL their first championship in more than 20 years. I had heard he was tyrannical in his methods, but I never paid much attention to the claim. He was hired by the best sports organization on the planet, in my mind, and so I was excited to work under him. I didn't mind if he was a bit of a hard-ass; I would do what it took to impress him and ultimately leave Fredericton in the rearview mirror for good.

I'll never forget my first day with the baby Habs — the day I met Therrien for the first time. We were playing a three-game rookie series against the baby Leafs in northern Ontario: the rinks were in New Liskeard, Timmins, and Kirkland Lake, I believe. In Timmins, I ate my pre-game meal with a few of the players I knew either from the "Dub" (WHL) or from camps previous. Early on in a year, a typical hockey team divides into cliques, and because young players are vulnerable to nerves, loneliness, and fatigue, good leadership is crucial. Brad Brown (a first-round draft choice in 1994), one of my good pals to this day and eventual captain of the 1997–98 Fredericton Canadiens, stood up next to me and invited a few European players over to sit with us and break the ice. I don't remember all of 'em, of course, but a few names sitting at our table stand out because they would end up being my teammates for a couple of years in Freddy Beach: Tomas Vokoun, Miloslav Guren, and Alexei Lojkin (I never heard Alexei, a Russian, say one word in any language unless he was drunk) joined myself, Brad, Matt Higgins (a first-rounder in 1996), and Boyd Olson.

I respected Brad as a leader. He knew that starting with a new team was especially tough on guys who didn't speak English or French well and who were a lot further from home than the rest of us. Brad, myself, and Matt identified with each other because we were Habs first-rounders. It was great to spend most of my time in Freddy Beach with those guys. The transition from minor hockey player to professional, from kid to adult, happens almost overnight. One minute you're making $60 a week and playing rock-paper-scissors with your roommate over who is popping the frozen pizza into the oven, and the next you are buying your parents an SUV and sampling the wine lists at five-star restaurants all over North America. It's surreal. The transition is even more intense when you're a high draft pick for a franchise like the Montreal Canadiens.

I am not complaining here—there are extreme highs and lows that come with the territory, and as many pros as cons. Without drifting too far off topic, it's obvious that the money, fame, and women are fantastic—but you need to know how to deal with those things, and it isn't something anyone prepares you for. Everyone wants a piece of you. One night a buddy and I picked up a couple of women at Thursday's after a game and took them to our hotel room. After we were done getting to know each other, they asked us for $500 each (or else) and I just about collapsed! We couldn't have been more innocent, and they knew what was going on all along.

My dad was able to teach me a lot as an ex-pro who played in the Ontario Hockey Association (now OHL) and the World Hockey Association, but Brad, Matt, and I were miles beyond that level of fame due to our association with the Canadiens. Fans in Montreal can be great because they are brutally honest—but a kid who isn't even old enough to drink legally in America doesn't necessarily react positively to every last piece of news reported about him. It was good to have each other to lean on and feed off of. Good leaders are often good listeners.

Anyhow, halfway through our staple meal of chicken, pasta, and veggies, we could smell smoke—someone had lit a cigarette. When we looked at the next table, Therrien was having a smoke after eating. I thought this was odd, not to mention unprofessional. (It may even have been illegal—I can't remember if smoking in a hotel conference room that served food was against the law back then, but I sure as hell know nobody else present would have had the balls to try to pull it off.) Mike noticed my glare of amazement and called me over to sit across from him. His accent remains drilled into my frontal lobe like a bad song that won't go away. It's a unique blend of French and English, with a dash of ignorance and narcissism, mixed with a chain-smoker's rasp. "Do you know why I am smoking?" he asked. "Because I fucking can—and I can send you down to the ECHL tomorrow."

This was it, my strange introduction to Michel Therrien. Shortly after, my outlook towards hockey would change. I wasn't so innocent anymore, and hockey wasn't so fun. My career was no longer a guarantee. By season's end, my 50 goals in one season of junior hockey were a distant memory. My determination lingered, but confidence came and went.

What emerged, however, was an unlikely new fighting leader in the AHL.

I've said it before: I don't want to blame my underachievement on anyone else. And I don't. It's my fault. I mean, ask any hockey player, they have lots of stories about this coach or that coach that may have given them the shaft. Most guys are bullshitting, but some guys have some truth to what they say. I take full responsibility for my career. I made some bad decisions and I deal with it. It's just more magnified for me personally as I come from a small province, and because of my achievement or lack thereof I am very recognizable. I am still involved in local sports as a player, coach, and fan and am very active in the community. This, combined with such a high draft placement and the fact that the team I was taken by was the Habs, makes everyone here in the local sporting world have an opinion, and that's okay. I made a lot of good friends in the game, and I am attracted to vibrant personalities with a zest for living. I tend to be positive-minded and I'm seldom serious; I make jokes at funerals, because it's my way of dealing with things. I had my ups and downs with Michel Therrien, but I think the thing that really stands out about him was the powerfully intimidating vibe he gave off. Under him I felt more like a soldier than an athlete.

Therrien smoked on the team bus. I don't mean he had a dart after games, before guys got out of the showers and onto the old iron lung. What I mean is, the guy treated the team bus like it was his fuckin' shed. It's about an hour and a half drive, tops, from Fredericton to Saint John—good ol' MT would suck back half a dozen smokes as we drove to the game.

The first time it happened I was in a state of disbelief. I looked over at Jonathan Delisle—God rest his soul—and Johnny's eyes were bigger than Mike's ego. He was so astonished, he couldn't stop laughing! I lost it and erupted in laughter as well. Mike could hear us but he couldn't see us because we were ducked down behind the seats in front of us holding our noses, turning red. As we tried to hold it in, I knew uproarious laughter was about to be unleashed at this, the worst of times, and tried desperately to hold it in and not do further damage to my career. I managed about as much restraint as Garfield in a lasagna factory. The next thing I knew I was unleashing snot and saliva all over the seat in front of me with an enormous sneeze. I was practically hysterical. The rest of the bus started to chuckle as well, but I took the heat. I guess I deserved it. When we were getting off the bus, Mike came real close to my face — so close I not only could smell cigarettes but could determine the shade of brown the cigarettes had made his once-pearly whites. He sat me down and said . . . nothing. He just stared at me, which was worse than any insult he could hurl. I admitted to him I was acting like a child. It was my fault, not Johnny's. If nothing else I was always a good teammate that way (most hockey players are); you can talk with any one of my teammates from over the years and I think they'll back me up on that. (My father taught me well when he told me to worry about myself before I go around yapping about others. He always said: Go hard on the ice and do the right thing off of it. It was that train of thought that persuaded my pappy to pursue the WHL in the first place. He said it was a "man's league.")

Michel was the only coach I have ever had that gave me "the tap" — who told me when to fight. He didn't do it all the time, and I'm definitely not implying that every fight involving one of his players is a direct result of him forcing players to drop the gloves, but he did it from time to time. To be honest, I really didn't mind it under most circumstances; I am merely stating the fact for the purpose of pointing out the extremes Mike will go to while on task. That gesture — telling a player to fight — is way more uncommon than many fans think. Not because coaches don't want their players mixing it up here and there, but because a player at that level usually knows when to go. Mike, however, had a way of bringing out your inner beast.

At the beginning of the '97–98 season, I was struggling and feeling the heat from all sides — coaches, friends, and family. I deserved it; I wasn't in the best shape at camp — my cardio was always good, but my strength training was hopeless before that season. I was lighter, so I felt fast (skating was my worst attribute and I figured slimmer meant faster), but clearly something was missing. To play my game well I needed to be strong. I scored my first goal in my eighth game and had an assist, so that game felt like a huge weight off my back. I was selected first star, and both fans in the Aitken Centre cheered (we never had much fan support). Wayne Gamble, the team's president, called me in and gave me a beer in his office — we are still pals today — and told me to relax. I called home, and I remember smiling as I chatted with Ma and Pa. The next night, we played the St. John's Leafs and I had only a few shifts all game, when all of a sudden towards the end I got the tap to go take on Jeff Ware, who was my age and Toronto's first-round selection the same year I was taken. Mike was making his point — he fuckin' owned me. He had total control and he knew it. He also knew I'd respond. Jeff was big and talented, but he wanted no part of it. We actually fought a couple of times professionally — I kicked his ass and he kicked mine, both in the Molson Centre — but not like this. I believe the officials saw what was happening and gave us double minors after the skirmish. Looking back, the move was horseshit on Mike's part, but at the time I was still doing anything to make the NHL, and he was a young coach too, learning as he went.

As the season progressed, I quickly realized that scrapping meant playing. The more I fought, the more I played. In junior, I was a scoring machine who got into the odd tilt. I was a good middleweight, I suppose, who fought the odd "heavy" if the team needed someone to step up. I don't think I ever expected to beat the real tough guys, but I knew how to stand in there and not get shit-hauled, and sometimes that's all you need to give your team a bit of momentum. I didn't have much fear on the ice, and that helps. Also, when an opponent knows you fight, he gives you a little more space, and that means more scoring opportunities. I wasn't a great hitter, but I finished my checks, and I kept a tough reputation by getting penalized for fighting. That year in the AHL, I had over 30 fighting majors and was one of the league leaders. I was on a line with my good buddy David Ling, and that felt comfortable. The thing is, Linger is all of 5-foot-8 and he chirps a lot, so trouble found me, often. Don't get me wrong, either; even if Kurt Browning had been my coach, I was good for 10 to 15 tilts that season. Grittiness was, after all, one of the reasons Demers and Savard, who were now long gone, had drafted me. It's just that Mike Therrien made it feel like part of the job. Things he said in the room made the ice feel like a battlefield. I could see what he was doing, but I hate that approach to the game, even though my style may not show it.

One night in Philly I remember grabbing Frankie "the Animal" Bialowas. Darcy Harris and I had played rock-paper-scissors on the bench right after the anthem, and I lost. It was the first shift and it was suicide, but we could tell Mike wanted it done. Fuck it, I was gonna be the guy to do it. I told Frankie I got a dance from his stripper girlfriend the night before, and felt the knuckles thrash my forehead milliseconds later. It was true, I had gotten a dance from some chick the boys told me was his girlfriend, but they could have been ruffling my feathers, and Frankie didn't give a shit anyway. He told me so in the penalty box while we served our time, and he bought me a beer after the game. I watched him growing up—he was one of my heroes when he played for the St. John's Leafs—so it was a memorable day for me.

Michel and I disliked each other; but oddly, I think we found a way to respect each other for most of the time we worked together. I kept him at a distance and he did the same to me. In his defence, I'm exuberant. I can be loud and obnoxious, I know, especially after a few wobbly-pops, but I think Mike always thought I was a partier in an addictive-type way, and that just wasn't the case. None of us were extreme boozers, but I am pretty sure he thought we were. We drank to listen to music and hit on women, like most young adults. Drugs were non-existent, save for the odd toke of weed at the year-end party. With some of the things I have been told over the years, and the things that leaked back to the Habs brass, I think they always thought there was more going on than there was.

I remember one house party—the whole team showed. We drank beer and listened to Gordie Dwyer's mix-tapes (he'd leave them with me when he got sent down to New Orleans, our farm team in the ECHL). It was a pretty typical Super Bowl shaker, but the next day Mike made a huge deal about it, and I took the fall. He knew I wouldn't sell anyone out, so when he asked me specifically who was there I said it was my friends from Newfoundland who were in town going to university. A few of the boys stepped up—I remember Darcy Harris, Dave Morissette, and Jose Theodore all explaining things, but it didn't matter.

My phone would ring at 11:05 (on a night when curfew was at 11)—shit like that. Mike kept a close eye on me, and to be honest I would have too; I think all my coaches did. It wasn't that I was a cancer (I would like to think I was the opposite), but I would do stupid shit. I was the guy who'd make a porn tape and show the boys. I was the guy who got up to sing at the bar. I needed to be the centre of attention, and each night out seemed destined to create another TR story. People talk, and I was always onstage, so to speak. The vast majority of the coaches in my past considered this a positive attribute—I knew how to walk the fine line and keep everyone in a loose mood; but in Montreal the line was foggy. This was partly because of the language barrier and partly because as the coach of the Fredericton Canadiens, Michel was, in a way, their top scout. If he didn't approve, I'm sure his progress reports weren't glowing.

I ended up living in fear of Michel, and hated being around the rink. The NHL seemed further away than ever. A turning point of sorts came during the playoffs of 1999. Eric Charron, the captain of the Saint John Flames, had been out of the lineup for months with some kind of disease, I think it had to do with his kidneys or something like that. At any rate, Eric had lost a lot of weight and was thought to be done for the season. When he appeared in the warm-up for game one, the fans gave him a standing ovation and there was a genuine good vibe to be felt in the rink.

When we got back into the room before the game, Mike asked me to take the wind out of their sails: he wanted me to rough him up, and although he never told me to specifically fight, it very much seemed implied. I thought he was joking, but Mike wasn't laughing. I looked at the assistant coach, my pal Gerry Fleming, disgusted, and I barked something at him and broke my stick over the wall. I was furious. Right there and then I mentally checked out of the Habs organization.

I went on the ice, skated for Charron, and told him to just go down as I wailed on the back of his helmet. As I was pummelling him, I apologized. This was out of character for me and fired me up for the wrong reasons. I was anything but dirty and I took pride in that, so I felt cheap. What made me feel worse was that as I skated off the fans weren't all that surprised by my actions. In junior hockey, our fans would have been mortified by my conduct out there. I was a fearless leader, not to be mistaken for a predatory cheap-shot artist. I told Eric I was just doing my job and I went in the dressing room, took off my gear, and had one of the best cries I had in years. I fired my gear all over the room and left it where it landed. I walked to the bus and listened to the Beatles on my Sony Discman as I sat alone in the dark and pondered my reputation. I was all that I didn't want to be. I wanted out, and I didn't care where I went or how I got there.

Growing Pains

One thing I want to point out before I move on is that I wish Michel Therrien the best, I really do. When it came time to publish this book, I toyed with the idea of leaving the previous section out, but then I'd be sugar-coating my story. Some people aren't gonna like it, but I don't give a shit. The fact is I forgive Michel and have moved on. I was hard to deal with at times too, I'm sure. We are actually very similar. We are both real stubborn and will go to great lengths to win. Michel knew the game inside out and I share most of the same core ideas concerning the game of hockey as he does. I don't think Michel understood sometimes how much he influenced a young player's practice, game, day, or week. His authoritarian tendencies seemed extreme to me and many others back then, but underneath the stern cloak he seemed to wear most of the time was a man focused on winning and surprisingly approachable at times.

My best memory with Michel Therrien is after a game in Providence one night in 1998. I had a charley horse in my right upper thigh and needed some help from our jubilant athletic trainer, Jacques Parent. I flung the door to his room open, assuming he'd be there already, but lo and behold I was in the wrong place. The only person in this particular room was Michel, and he sat alone half undressed on one of the beds, thinking about the loss we had to the Bruins that night. He had a playbook in front of him. There was a bucket on the floor with some beers in it, and Michel offered me one so I took it. I used the ice in the bucket on my thigh and we sat and shot the shit for the full third period of whatever NHL game was on TV that particular evening. I have no idea who was playing in the game we watched, but I remember our entire conversation and recall thinking to myself Michel was a lot more human than I had imagined.

We had a few of those instances, and that's one of the reasons I hold no grudge against the guy. After all, he was a rookie coach, as I was a rookie player, and one tends to learn a lot from experience. If nothing else, he was as passionate as I was about the game of hockey, and I respect that. As I watched the playoffs in 2013 and Michel was being interviewed in the Habs/Senators series after some very complicated circumstances, I realized he had matured as a coach. I may not necessarily ever be the man's best pal, but then again we are all different people and life goes on. We build character from adverse situations and grow from them.

I'm still a Habs fan and Mike is their coach. I feel a sense of accomplishment after writing this, like a chapter of my life closed and I can move on. Now, as they say in *la belle province — bonne chance, Les Habitants!*

He's a Bird Dog

As long as I am on the topic of the Fredericton Canadiens, it would be remiss of me not to mention a story about one of the looniest tunes ever to lace up a pair of skates, Greg "Bird Dog" Smyth. Bird Dog is 6-foot-4, 240, in shape, and doesn't always say much, but when he does, everyone listens. He likes to drink his cold ones early in the afternoon and voice his opinions when he gets sloppy drunk. When he played, he used his stick like an axe, was never clean-shaven, and never went one full season without being suspended. Bird Dog went 22nd overall, and most of that was based on pure meanness, which means the fucker was pretty goddamn mean. He played 228 NHL games for Philly, Quebec, Florida, Calgary, Chicago, and Toronto. He is from Mississauga but lives in St. John's now, not far from me, and dresses in rubber boots and flannel jackets more than any Newfoundlander I know. In Newfoundland terms, he looks like a "Bayman." Bird and I became friends over time after he settled down in Newfoundland after finishing his playing career here in the late 1990s playing for the St. John's Maple Leafs. Telling just one story about Bird Dog doesn't do his legend justice, but I'll do the best I can in the short space provided. If I ever write another book and need a topic, the life and times of Bird Dog is on my short list!

I first played against Bird Dog in an exhibition game in New Liskeard, northern Ontario. The Leafs rookies played the Habs rookies in a three-game series of exhibition contests. Each team dressed one or two veterans, and the rest of the lineups were young fellas full of piss and vinegar, vying for minor-league contracts. A select few like me knew we were going to be playing in the AHL that season, but we were still auditioning for a future spot in the NHL. Scouts were plentiful and the games were intense.

I remember playing those games every year as a prospect. I recall certain players on opposing teams—like P.J. Stock, Eric Boulton, and Jody Shelley—playing extra-hard and being rewarded for their determination by signing NHL deals. The level of violence in these games was high, even for the tough guys. Most games ended in bloodbaths and produced way more fights than any regular match, but what do you expect when people are fighting for a job? I hated playing in those circumstances, but everyone had to do it, and if nothing else, you quickly found out who had your back. Playing in tiny rinks, fighting for guys you barely know in small northern towns like New Liskeard added butterflies to an already nerve-racking situation. So here we were starting our second game of the exhibition swing. All I can remember about the first game is that it was in Timmins and I fought Shawn Thornton—who was a late draft pick by Toronto but made St. John's as a result of taking on all comers during exhibition—a couple of times. Bird Dog wasn't dressed for game one, but as the anthem played in New Liskeard I could see him on the bench and I got stomach sick. I'm not kidding! I wanted Bird Dog to play that game like I wanted a sack of hammers across the jaw.

As I hopped the boards for my first shift, I skated right at Bird. The whistle had gone and I looked him in the eye as we were getting ready for the faceoff and told him I'd fuckin' fight him if I had to. I wanted to take the shit-kicking early and worry about hockey after that. I said I wouldn't disrespect him out there, but I didn't want to be suckered either. Bird looked at me and never said shit, which made me feel worse. Halfway through the shift, I cut down his side and had him almost beat when he slashed me in the back of the ankle and put me out of the game.

Our resident vet, Gerry Fleming, told me not to buzz down Bird Dog's side anymore. "That's fucking ridiculous, Flemmer," I said. "I'm not letting a fucking guy own me like that; I don't give a fuck who he is."

That's when Gerry gave me some good advice. "Sometimes Terry, you have to cool it and realize there are bigger, much tougher players out there and you have to know how to play against them. Bird Dog is an extremely physical presence, it's his best attribute. Having physical altercations with guys like that will give the other team momentum every time. We love your balls, but we don't wanna lose games because we are too anxious and undisciplined either. And that goes for any team you play on. There's a time and a place for everything, and if nothing else, Greg Smyth respects you now, I guarantee it."

That was the beginning of the 1997–98 season, which would end up being my first in the AHL. By the end of my second year, I had played against Bird Dog many times because the St. John's Leafs were in our division. Flemmer was right on the money; Bird must have respected me a little, because he never really came at me to fight in those two years. Indeed, he slashed me, elbowed me, hooked me, held me, and cross-checked me hundreds of times, but never dropped his gloves with me, and that suited me just fine. That isn't to say, however, he never lost his marbles here and there.

In the '99 playoffs, we were up 2–0 on St. John's in a best-of-five division final, coming back to Fredericton. We had played well on the Rock and had the Leafs in a bind. Arron Asham and Jose Theodore played awesome that series, and we also had a strengthened lineup; major junior call-ups Jason Ward, Mike Ribeiro, and Eric Chouinard were now playing with us, as their seasons had ended. All was well in Freddy Beach.

As we wound down our pre-game skate on the day of game three, some of our guys stayed on the ice to get some extra practice. Now-household names Mathieu Garon and Tomas Vokoun backed up Theodore, so they were also on the ice getting some extra shots in order to stay sharp in case Theo went down with an injury. I was just entering the dressing room ready to take my gear off after our skate and head to McGinnis Landing, our favourite restaurant in town. As I laid my wooden Sherwood Feather-Lite on the stick rack, I heard big Moose Morissette yell "Duck!" followed by loud thuds every two or three seconds. Our dressing room door was around a corner and about 50 feet from the ice, so as I made my way out there I had no idea what to expect. I thought someone was using a hammer on the bench maybe.

When I turned the corner I saw a puck fly by my face and I took Moose's advice and hit the deck under our bench. Pucks were everywhere. Me, Moose, Ash, and Olson were literally on our stomachs under our player's bench, staring at each other, and I was still mystified. It was like we were soldiers in a trench. I looked at Moose. "Moose, what in the fuck is going on out there?"

"Bird Dog is going cra-zee," Moose uttered in his French-English accent. "He is shooting pucks at us, skating around our ice!"

I peeked out over the bench and sure enough, Moose wasn't lyin'. Bird had emptied out a bucket of pucks and was shooting them at us, telling us it was their turn to practise. He wasn't doing it for show, either—he was trying to hit us, not warn us. "Your time is up, assholes," he yelled. "Get the fuck off our ice."

The last shot I saw grazed Rollie Melanson's leg as he dashed out of the way, and all of our guys came off the ice. Apparently we had gone over our time . . . by one minute. The rink attendant was late blowing the horn to get us off the ice, and Bird took exception.

That night I was floored to see ol' Bird Dog skating around in warm-up, with no bucket on, chirping at our supporters as they beaked him from the stands. Bird Dog even shot a few pucks up at a couple of fearless fans who had the balls to stick their heads over the glass. I was flabbergasted the maniac wasn't suspended. My feelings see-sawed back and forth between admiration and disbelief. He was a true beauty.

That series ended up being one for the ages. We beat St. John's by a goal in game five in their barn—old Memorial Stadium—after much on- and off-ice conflict. Mark Deyell (one of their best forwards and a buddy of mine from the WHL) lost an eye with an accidental stick to the face in game three, and emotions escalated. The night before the deciding game five on the Rock, star Leafs forward Lonny Bohonos and Michel Therrien (amongst others) were involved in a barroom fight at Turkey Joe's on George Street, which was the club the Leafs tended to frequent in those days. To say that Lonny didn't like our coach would be an understatement. They were always yelling at each other on the ice, so it wasn't a total shock to see the hatred spill over into the bar. So many stories surrounded the incident; nobody will really know what went down other than those involved. Most of our players were back at the hotel, and when we got up for breakfast in the morning we realized it was war as we heard Michel's version of the story. We battled hard for him, and rightly so. At the sound of the buzzer, Michel ordered us to get off the ice and ignore the traditional handshake. He was still furious and wanted this grudge to continue. I wanted to move on. I grabbed a half dozen Habs or so and we shook hands anyway, although we'd all spend the rest of the year in the doghouse.

I don't necessarily agree with him, but I do see where he was coming from. We are just two different people. I have always separated the game from my personal life, and maybe that's harder for Michel to do. He bleeds hockey and winning, it's everything to him. Like I have been known to say before, I think if someone could combine my best qualities with Michel's best qualities, you'd have one helluva hockey personality.

From Long Beach to Utah to St. John's
1999–2000

By the time the next season rolled around, I was adamant: I was not returning to the Montreal Canadiens. In June, after I expressed how I felt to my agent, he let me know he'd do what he could to help—he understood the situation. He'd contact some teams after letting the Habs know we wanted to part ways, and that would be that. I'd get a chance with another club and they'd get something in return.

It sounded great, but things didn't work out that way.

When September came, I was still waiting for a trade and training daily with the University of Alberta Golden Bears. I'd skate with the guys and then grab lunch and call Mike Barnett, every day. I stayed with Ryan Marsh, the Bears captain, and although Marshy and I had a fantastic couple of months getting reacquainted and reliving junior memories, I was starting to worry about where I'd play. As September rolled on and training camps came to a close, I knew I had to do something. If I wasn't playing hockey at a high level, I'd become yesterday's news—and who's kidding who, it'd also be nice to earn a paycheque after a long summer.

Finally, Mike called and told me to go to the airport. I was heading to Long Beach, California, to play for the Ice Dogs, he said, but my stay might not be long.

He was correct.

I played one game for Long Beach—had a minor skirmish with Daniel Lacroix—and after the game I had a meeting with the coach, John Van Boxmeer. Boxy told me there was a logjam of players at left wing and I'd be of better use elsewhere. He wished me luck and told me I'd be heading to Utah in the morning to play for the Grizzlies. That night the whole Los Angeles area and I experienced an earthquake of more than seven on the Richter scale. The hotel room I stayed in swayed from side to side, and I was knocked out of bed in the process. I had no idea what was happening until I turned on the television. My cell phone rang—my mom was apparently also watching back in Mount Pearl, worried about my safety. Soon she'd be able to check on my safety on a daily basis. It wasn't long before I found myself living at home.

I played a month in Utah, and although I loved everything about it, I was happy when Glenn Stanford called me from back home. He was the GM of the St. John's Maple Leafs and was interested in my services for the remainder of the season. After losing a few players in early October, the Leafs had some openings up front. My rights wouldn't be owned by the Leafs, unfortunately, but I'd be performing in front of oodles of scouts on a nightly basis, and I'd be playing home games in front of my hometown fans—a nice bonus. From a hockey perspective, I was happy with my decision to leave Utah. Long Beach and Utah were International Hockey League teams back then, and that league was filled with older guys—many of whom had already peaked. Little buzz surrounded the league, to be honest.

The one thing I would miss would be the scenery of Salt Lake. It is a beautiful city, surrounded by mountains, rivers, lakes—one of the most picturesque places in the USA. The religious element is a little over the top, however. At the time, the liquor laws were very strict, and you needed a membership to get into a drinking establishment. I think it's changed, but in 1999 it was harder to buy a beer in Utah than it was to buy a gun. When I asked people why, at least half the time, "God" was part of the answer. I believe good things happen to good people when they die and all that, but sometimes religion really pisses me off, especially the extremists. Most blind faith is nonsense, even creepy. All these holier-than-thou groups and sects inventing rules to live by, trying to lure people in by promising a great afterlife; meanwhile millions of people in human history have died early deaths in the name of religion. Telling me I'm not going to "Heaven" because I smoked weed at a rock concert or had sex before I was married. Thinking my uncle Daryl is inferior because he's gay. Fuck that hypocrisy. I'm technically Catholic, and when I was a kid I could never understand why I'd have to go confess my sins to some old man in a booth. We had to do it in school! Schools in Newfoundland were denominational (separated by religion) until the mid-1990s, and having to go to "Confession" would send me on a rant every time we had to do it. I'd think, doesn't this priest sin? Well, it turns out many religious leaders in powerful positions *did* sin, now, didn't they, and we all know how that went. I was a kid, feeling bad for getting into a fight on school grounds over a G.I. Joe action figure, and some people I was confessing to were jerking off ten-year-old boys who couldn't defend themselves, scarring their minds for the rest of their lives. A load of bullshit. Do to others as you'd want done to you. Be a good, unselfish person for the good of humanity, end of story. If there's a God, he, she, or it will take notice, I promise.

If You Can't Beat 'Em . . .

St. John's is a fantastic place to play hockey. Even if I weren't a Newfoundland native, I'd want to play on the Rock. The city is picturesque and people are friendly—hockey players love it because they are treated like celebrities in our small, but big-enough, city of 200,000. I played at Memorial Stadium—an old barn with a lot of character—but today AHL games are played at Mile One Centre. It is located right downtown, and the world-famous George Street is a stone's throw away. Most people around town recognize the hockey pros and are accommodating in every kind of way. Once you're playing for our city, representing our province, you're treated like a native son. People are genuinely proud of their team and support it well. The baby Leafs are long gone at this point, but we have the Winnipeg Jets' minor league affiliate playing here now—the St. John's Ice Caps. They sell out consistently, benefitting not only from the loyal local support but also from the most prosperous economy we've seen since Joey Smallwood led us into Confederation in 1949.

Playing for the baby Leafs, I had a decent year as a grinder on the third line. Because I wasn't signed with Toronto, I had to be ready to play whatever role they needed me for—guys who are on independent contracts fill voids. For most of the season I played with Aaron Brand and Ryan Pepperall. Brando and Pepps were good lineys; we showed up, worked hard, and did what we were told. Pepps and I were roomies on the road and spent many nights finishing a case of beer while sitting in our room after games icing injuries while watching sports highlights and talkin' about what the hell we were gonna do with the rest of our lives. Simple stuff, but I savoured every minute. I also truly enjoyed our coaches that season: Al MacAdam and Dave Cameron. Al is a tall, slender man with silvery hair who tells many entertaining stories from his experiences in the NHL. He played nearly 900 games with Philadelphia, Cleveland, California, Minnesota, and Vancouver. Dave played a few years in the bigs with Colorado and New Jersey but is known today more for his coaching prowess; he is now the assistant coach of the Ottawa Senators and after a stellar OHL coaching career led Canada's World Junior team to a silver medal in 2011 in Buffalo, New York. Both gents are good Prince Edward Islanders I'm proud to call friends.

St. John's was fun, but also very busy for me. I had dozens of friends and family members at each home game, and it felt nice to see my home through a wintery lens for the first time in nearly a decade. I was so busy that I rarely wrote anything in my journal, and the scribblings I did manage were just notes. Many stories from that time flood my memory, but I really want to talk about my pal Shawn Thornton. His work ethic and focus are to be respected and admired, because this kid started out the most unlikely of candidates to make the world's best hockey league. It still fascinates me how successful Thorty has become — but it doesn't surprise me.

When I was with the baby Habs and first played against the baby Leafs, Thornton looked awful on the ice. He couldn't pass well, his positioning left something to be desired, and his shot was average. He could skate fast in a straight line but he turned like a 747. He made the baby Leafs after playing with extreme intensity at camp and doing what he was told. We fought a couple of times in northern Ontario at Leafs/Habs rookie exhibition games (these games tend to get violent), and I can tell you first-hand he throws hard. Basically, Shawn used the limited tools he had to make an impact and ended up signing a very low-end AHL deal. If you had told me back then he'd make the NHL someday, I'd have called you a fool. By the time

I got to St. John's three years later, however, Thorty had come a long way. When we played against each other we often got into fights, but as usual the mutual respect between fighters paved the way for a great friendship.

We hung out every day in St. John's. Me, Pepps, Thorty, D.J. Smith, Adam Mair, and Donald "Daddy Mac" MacLean would hit a place after practice for a beer and a bite—usually it'd be a pub like Kelly's, O'Reilly's, or Green Sleeves, and depending on the circumstances and scenery we might even end up staying for a couple of hours and hittin' up the Sundance Saloon a little later, which was often jammed for happy hour. If we drank a little too hard, Thorty would always be the first one at the rink in the morning, riding the bike and sweating out the booze before our skate. "Don't hang with the men at night if you're gonna act like a boy in the morning," he'd say. Thorty always seemed to lift my spirits, even at the worst of times.

Once, I took a girl home from a bar in Quebec City and she robbed me. I fell asleep after eight seconds of ultimate pleasure, and the chick cleaned me out. She left my credit card and a thank-you note, though, which I appreciated. The thing is, I deserved it. I actually had a $1000 bill in my wallet I'd use for comedic purposes. I'd wrap it in fives as I ordered drinks and make sure hot women saw it. It was a ridiculous pick-up move, but the success rate was high, and that was the main thing. When I told Thorty about my monetary loss the next morning, he took me out for lunch. We ended up going to a comedy club in Hamilton that night with a few of the boys and had a great time. He paid for my share. It was all a laugh, and obviously it was my fault, but the point is, Thorty seemed to use the slightest bit of adversity to bring a team together. This attribute can easily be dismissed, but it is one of the keys to a successful team.

When the season ended, we finished dead last. We had only 23 wins in 80 games—out of the playoffs and onto the golf course right away. Still, it was comforting for me to play at home after so much adversity. As a team we could have been better, but there is no doubt that guys like Thorty, Adam Mair, and Kevyn Adams used the experiences we shared that season to their advantage en route to success at a higher level. My mom slept a little easier each night, and my buddies got free tickets to every home game and hung out with some future NHL stars. One thing I loved about that season was being on the home side of Brian Rogers's radio call. He's from the Rock and is one of the best in the business. I looked up to Brian like I had looked up to Red Fisher before Red treated me like shit. "Rog" is my Foster Hewitt and is as colourful now, working for the St. John's Ice Caps, as he was in 1983, when he first got a gig with VOCM, a local radio station here in St. John's.

As for Thorty? Well, he kept working his nuts off. He put up 320 penalty minutes the next season, scrapping anyone who stepped in the path of a teammate or his NHL dream. In 2002–03 Shawn finally got to suit up for the Chicago Blackhawks, playing in 13 games for the historic club that season. It didn't hurt that Al MacAdam was an assistant coach in Chicago by that time—he knew how focused and determined his young disciple really was. All the hard work was paying dividends, and over the next two seasons he played 31 more games for the Hawks. Mission accomplished, right? Wrong. Shawn Thornton now has two Stanley Cup rings. He found himself in Anaheim in 2006–07 and played a small but important role in their quest for the Cup. He played on the fourth line with energy and enthusiasm and inspired his teammates through leading by example. I wasn't surprised; these were always obvious attributes. He is a warrior. In 2011, Thorty won another Stanley Cup, this time as a member of the Boston Bruins, and played an even bigger role in the big win. In his mid-30s, the guy is still improving, and he's a great example for any young kid. Congrats, Thorty, and fly me down for your next Cup celebration, will ya? God knows you have at least one left in you.

Me at nine; I was always a Habs fanatic! On the back, my jersey says “Nilan.”

Me, my dad, and my grandfather in 1986; Dad just coached the Mount Pearl Jr. Blades to provincial and Atlantic Jr. B championships. I watched every game and skated at every practice.

The Mount Pearl PeeWee Blades in 1990 after Sean Gibbons scored in double overtime at the provincial winter games. I won MVP at the Atlantic Championship a month later. (My mom is GM, far right.)

The draft is still surreal! Such a flood of emotions; my parents' sacrifice and my hard work had paid off unimaginably. That's Gary Bettman, Andre Boudrias, me, and Doug Robinson.

Three first rounders! That's me with Tri-City teammates Daymond Langkow and Brian Boucher. We will always be close due to these unique experiences at such a young age.

Mom and me before my first NHL camp. She stayed behind the scenes, but without her support I'd never have achieved my hockey dreams. Thanks Mom!

Playing at Maple Leaf Gardens in 1996. I loved the freedom of playing with no visor.

© Graig Abel / Graig Abel Collection

After the 1995 CHL All-Star game in Kitchener. I had a highlight goal and a fight; my stock rose overnight. A great memory because I realized I could play with the best.

RIP Mike Collins. In Quesnel, Mike was a big brother—he protected me. We'd have a few beers and he'd plan my career! I miss you, Mike.

Arron Asham. We were roomies in junior and pro; he's such a good role player that people forget he had over 40 goals twice in junior. He oozes character, a great team guy.

© Juan Salas / Icon SMI

Michel Therrien and I didn't see eye to eye, but in hindsight we were both rookies at our trade. We had some major battles, but I've moved on and wish him well.

© Minas Panagiotakis / Icon SMI

Scrapping at home against arch-rival Spokane Chiefs in the 1995 WHL playoffs.

Many of my fights weren't wins or losses, they were toe-to-toe bouts that usually entertained the crowd. No exception here, in 1996 versus Lethbridge.

The late Wade Belak was throwing his weight around so I challenged him from the bench. After our fight, he came to my dressing room, chatted, and shook my hand. Class act.

© R.E. Huelsman / Terry Ryan Collection

In action for the Cincinnati Cyclones in 2002. Shortly afterwards, I hung my skates up professionally due to injuries. I was devastated.

After the 2010 Juno Awards in St John's, Dani and I got buzzed in Blue Rodeo's suite. Jim sent me this pic afterwards with a signed copy of *Outskirts*!

Winning the World Ball Hockey championship in Sierre, Switzerland, in 2003. No. 41 in the back is current Vancouver Canuck Alexandre Burrows, who won MVP of the tournament.

My wonderful family at home in Newfoundland in January 2013: Tison, Danielle, me, and Penny-Laine.

We usually join our good pals in PEI in the summer for a weekend of charity golf and fun. That's Ron MacLean and Brad Richards in the front—fantastic fellas.

© Brian Tuck

Senior hockey is huge in Newfoundland and very competitive. Games are a community event. This is our team picture right after the Conception Bay Comeback in 2013.

Hoisting the historic Herder Memorial trophy in 2013 as a member of the legendary Conception Bay CeeBees. Alex Faulkner, Newfoundland's first NHLer, was a CeeBee in the '50s and '60s.

© Brian Tuck

Colorado Gold Kings and Hershey Bears
2000–01

Bad to the Bone

When I was growing up in Mount Pearl, my buddies and I would hang around my basement while my dad had his drinkin' pals over on Friday nights. We'd listen in on the music they were listening to, and then we'd play these songs in the dressing room for everyone else to hear, so most of my pals had tastes that were on the odd side of normal for kids our age. My dad was into classic rock and had a huge collection. It was the 1980s, and even then the Beatles, Stones, Zeppelin, and Pink Floyd were a little dated, but we knew all their stuff. We also knew more rare but important artists like Buddy Holly and Badfinger inside out. Not a Friday would go by where we didn't hear good ol' George Thorogood, usually well into the night. George was fairly popular amongst adult rockers at the time, but not kids. None of my peers aside from my hockey buddies had heard of him. His hits, like "One Bourbon, One Scotch, One Beer" and "I Drink Alone," were a little out of our realm of understanding, to be honest.

During the 2000–01 hockey season, I got to meet Thorogood, while in San Diego playing for the Colorado Gold Kings of the now defunct West Coast Hockey League.

It was September 2000, and I remember being pissed off at my place in the hockey world. I was at a good enough level to be considered professional, but way off the radar for most NHL clubs needing immediate help. I'd been a role player in St. John's, but at least I was in the AHL, one step from the Show. Now, with a tricky contract situation and the fact that I'd refused to go back to Montreal's camp the year before, I found myself between the Rock and a hard place. The Habs were putting the blocks to me, and rightfully so. I'd made the rash decision to sit out of camp a year previous, and therefore the Habs owned and, well, buried me. I had fewer options than a Greenpeace-loving vegetarian at an oil and gas union workers' hot dog roast.

The thought of AA hockey had never entered my mind. Basically, at the time, the IHL and the AHL were the AAA-calibre leagues, one step away from the big time. Anybody playing elsewhere — the ECHL, CHL, WCHL, WPHL, ACHL, SPHL — was very far removed from a call-up.

My good pal Todd Gillingham was heading down to Colorado Springs to play for the Gold Kings of the West Coast Hockey League. Gilly was from the Rock too and had been around the game for a decade and a half. He is one of the characters hockey's famous for. With his 6-foot-3, 220 build and long, flowing dark brown hair, Gilly was always chewing what seemed like a whole pack of gum while he played and chirped the players, refs, and fans — pretty much anyone in the building was fair game. Gilly made a living in front of the net and yapped at players from the bench, getting them off their games and scrapping with them when it was called for. He was a big, imposing physical presence and had a decent scoring touch; his 26 goals and more than 400 PIMs in one year with Long Beach in the IHL are still impressive. Gilly couldn't skate a lick but had a very keen awareness out there and to this day is one of the top five passers I have seen in any league. He could make a one-armed pirate a 30-goal scorer just by banking pucks in off his stick.

Gilly made a call to Kirk "Gunner" Tomlinson, who was an old pal from his early days as a pro and then became head coach of the Gold Kings, and we soon made the trek to Colorado. I was tripping over my bottom lip at first, pissed off at my situation in an inferior league. My attitude soon changed. After a few days I realized the place was awesome! So many pros were playing down there and enjoying it. Flights, fans, weather, and free accommodations. In the American Hockey League we would bus everywhere, and we also paid our own room and board — at the time, the AHL cities were mostly located across the Eastern Seaboard, in and around the Atlantic Canada and New England region, so that mode of travel made sense. But the cities in the WCHL were diverse and distant, so we needed to fly to games. The contracts were paid per week, not per year, and of course that was a con. A guy could be cut at any time and find himself without work. I figured I was safe, though; I worked hard and kept in shape and was used to the pace of the AHL, and I was right. It was a good fit. I told Gunner I'd park the shitty attitude I came there with and give him everything I had.

I think it was about seven or eight games in, and I was still in awe. We were in the midst of a two-week road swing that saw us touch down in Fresno, Long Beach, San Diego, Phoenix, and Bakersfield. Only one practice was scheduled the entire trip. It was the big kahuna of all the road trips I had ever been on, and we were only at the season's dawn.

One particular afternoon, we were enjoying a day off in sunny San Diego, and the beach was hopping. Myself, Craig "Leo" Lyons,

Jeff "Sirk" Sirkka, and Zac "Z-Man" Boyer had an unobstructed view of the scenery from one of the local restaurants that acted as a border between the city and the surf. As I closed in on the last of my fistful of doubles (we were getting bamboozled), I noticed a familiar face staring back at me from across the bar. I was squinting, and even an hour earlier I would have officially blown over the legal limit, but I was still certain I was looking at a legend.

"Boys," I said, "That is George Thorogood."

No response.

"Did you fellas hear me?" I said.

"Ya, ya, whatever, T Bone," Lucky Leo, our fearless leader and captain of the ship said. "We aren't shit-faced yet. That definitely isn't Thorogood."

"I'm goin' over," I said.

And with that I got up from my seat and decided to approach one of my heroes. I wasn't sloppy drunk but I was close — buzzed enough to have confidence and make a fool of myself, but sober enough to successfully look up facts in my mental Rolodex.

George and his five o'clock shadow sat at the bar in a well-worn pair of cowboy boots and a white T-shirt, drinking what looked like a high-ball with a couple of empty shooter glasses within arm's length. There were two or three other people with him, but he seemed approachable. I nervously sat down and introduced myself, telling him how big a fan I was — not only of his songs but of many genres of music. After a well-savoured drink and a short chat, he shook my hand and wished me the best. I was elated. Leaving his company I felt fulfilled — I'd had a meaningful conversation with an idol.

As I got up to leave, George Thorogood asked if I wanted another drink. I figured he'd heard my answer more times than Al Capone during the Prohibition, but I went for it anyway.

"Mr. Thorogood," I said with the cocky confidence of Sean Avery after a big fight or goal, "I'll have a bourbon, a Scotch, and a beer!"

"Nice answer, kid. I'll get the drinks, but I'll have you know I've heard that one before," he said with a chuckle, and when they came he was only too happy to hand them over and pay the bill. However, George was puzzled as I took my drinks and sauntered away, rejoining my hockey pals across the bar.

"Hey, where you goin'?" George said, mystified.

"Well, here's the thing. I had a great time and I'd love to stay. You're a class act and a genuinely great guy," I said in my haze, "but unfortunately . . . I drink alone!"

With that, Thorogood burst into laughter. As much as I would have enjoyed going back, like George Costanza I had made the perfect exit and decided to keep it that way. The fellas howled, and I gazed out into the warm California sun, in disbelief at what had just happened. We had all been drinking, but deep down I know the glaze that covered my eyes was at least partly due to tears of joy thinking of the times I had spent with my family and my buddies at 45 Park Avenue in Mount Pearl.

It Hasn't Hit Me Yet

After meeting Thorogood, I never thought I'd have another moment like it. Over the years, however, I have met some great musicians who are intriguing people; some famous, some not. Tommy Thayer (Kiss), Robin Zander (Cheap Trick), Tom Cochrane, and Matty Shafer (a.k.a. Uncle Kracker) are maybe the most famous dudes I have been fortunate enough to sit down and have a beer with — and they were all good lads with legendary stories. Kracker and his pal and bandmate Mike Adkins sat with my dad, my wife, and my cousin Mike Tulk and chatted about Dad's playing days with the Kalamazoo Wings—Kracker and Adkins are from Michigan—until the bar closed one night in central Newfoundland after a concert; a fantastic memory. Bands like Great Big Sea, the Navigators, Brothers in Stereo, and the Irish Descendants are acquaintances back on the Rock, and they've influenced my life in many ways. Brian Byrne, the multi-tattooed, long-bearded, biker-lookin' lead singer of I Mother Earth (and critically acclaimed solo artist) is a guy I could sit and drink with for three periods any day. Great guy, great banter.

I seem to identify with musicians, for some reason. I tend to be a liberal thinker, I suppose, and that helps. There are many similarities between the hockey life and the music life; the group-road atmosphere and performing in front of thousands are two quick examples that come to mind, but there are more if you dig deep. I've always had a passion for music that's at least paralleled my passion for hockey; I've just never had the time to learn an instrument. Had I learned to play, I know I would have been hooked. Bob Dylan, Paul McCartney, and Bruce Springsteen are far more interesting to me than any athlete.

My plan is to get my buddies Chris LeDrew, Tino Borges, and Jeff Martin to teach me guitar. Tino runs a great little pub called the Bull and Barrel, which plays fantastic rock 'n' roll music, features talented musicians in an intimate setting, and is nestled comfortably into downtown St. John's. The Bull is one of my favourite watering holes. Chris, Tino, and Jeff have all had personal success as musicians and play in a killer local band called the Insiders. I'm like a fuckin' groupie—I drink where they play, and then we continue until the sun comes up. (I told the boys one night I'd find a relevant way to get them in the book . . . and there it is, boys.)

One of my closest friends in the music business is the man I call J Cud—Jim Cuddy. Most people know him as one of the frontmen—along with Greg Keelor—of Blue Rodeo. He's one of the best singer-songwriters this country has ever produced, is recognized by millions, and has the respect of some of the greatest musicians alive today. Yet when you meet him and make small talk, you get the feeling that he is genuinely interested in what you have to say—because he is. He's usually smiling, and his positive vibe is invaluable and contagious. A few years back, the Juno Awards (Canada's version of the Grammys) were held here on the Rock, and every year at the Junos, Jim raises money for MusiCounts—an educational charity associated with the Canadian Academy of Recording Arts and Sciences—by hosting a celebrity hockey game. On one side are musicians—some nominated for Junos and others who just want to play some stick—while the other squad is made up of former pros. I was at Blue On Water having a steak and a pint with local entrepreneur/tough guy/drinkin' buddy Jason Brake in the mid-afternoon, when I got a call from Kenny Marshall, who was helping to organize. "Hey Tee," he said, "some of the boys never got in—the fuckin' fog is like pea fuckin' soup. Suit up, kid!"

Apparently, legends like Mark Messier and Paul Coffey were "fogged out," as we Newfoundlanders say. At times, the fog gets so unbelievably dense that planes cannot get in or out of our airport. I am sure this happens in other places, but I would bet St. John's is one of the worldwide leaders in flight delays. Even if it is a wicked kinda day here in St. John's—the sun may feel Floridian and the asphalt may feel Georgian—if you see the fog rolling in over the banks surrounding the harbour, you may as well pack everything up and take the fastest route back to your couch and TV. When the blanket of dense grey haze slips in between the vibrant city and the blue sky, sandboxes empty, birds stop chirpin', and pubs fill up faster than you can say "Jiggs' dinner."

Sounds gloomy to an outsider, I'm sure. We've been bred, however, to not only accept the weather but embrace it. The way we see it, if the weather was nice all the time, too many people would move here.

Folks here are over-friendly and built with character, but that's no fluke, it's in our genes. Newfoundlanders are tough; we're used to adversity — hell, our descendants lived in this crappy climate since the 1600s, drawing on their survival instincts to protect their families. A new land of opportunity presented itself in a place saturated with fish but unpredictable in weather. While others left for the much more inviting climates down south, the tough bastards that would be our ancestors remained, built houses in the bays and on the sides of cliffs — open to hurricane winds, sleet, drizzle, snow, rain, hail, and fog — in order to prosper. They had to stay close and trust each other with their lives. What's amazing is that we have been around the longest, yet we haven't changed a great deal (in comparison with other provinces and states) as far as culture goes. Our heritage is very important to us. The same names can be found in the same communities. Traditions and family values remain important, and wherever you go, people are always willing to help. I am so passionate about my home that I've gone off topic again, but fuck it, this is my first book and that's gonna happen from time to time.

After I got the call to play, I called Francis "Moondawg" Mooney and told him I was in the lineup (he is a Blue Rodeo fan) and he made some calls and snagged a few tickets for my family and my buddies. I then told my wife, Danielle, about my "good fortune as a result of other people's bad fortune" and we high-fived and she started to get Tison ready — he was nine at the time — so he could come watch me skate with some of my idols. At the rink, all was good. A few of my local chums, other ex-NHLers, were playing as well; Bird Dog was in the house, as well as Harold "Drukes" Druken and Andrew "Mayday" McKim.

We played the game and had a blast. Drukes, McKim, and I played on a line, and Bird—still proving he didn't like people beating him down the wing—took a couple of slashing penalties on our good buddy actor Allan Hawco, of *Republic of Doyle* fame. It was par for the course: Bird Dog, as I mentioned in an earlier chapter, is one of the most feared players to ever lace up hockey skates professionally.

We all came together in the dressing room post-game and got half bamboozled before a bus picked us up and took us downtown to the Sheraton Hotel. When we got there, J Cud came right over to me and Moondawg and talked our ears off. He said he can identify with a hockey player who played in the minors because until he was in his 30s he worked other jobs. He was always writing and performing, but it took some time to become a professional musician who could support a family through just his music. I told him about my massive vinyl collection—amongst other things—and we called my buddy Pops Howell, who owned a convenience store, and he set us up with 20 dozen beer. Moondawg went to grab Pops and his beer and we filled the bathtubs of the adjoining suites the boys had rented with beer and ice. I'd gone back to school and had an exam the next day, in Geography 1000, but Danielle and I agreed: this was a unique opportunity and too much fun. I was half buzzed, with my shirt off, singing with Jim Cuddy in front of a room filled with artistic talent. I didn't deserve to be there, but I was enjoying the ride (Danielle was looking smokin', and I am sure that took some sting off my obnoxiousness).

We got home after the sun had risen, and I went into my exam with a 78 percent grade and came out of it with 65. Doing the math, I must have gotten somewhere around 25 percent on the final. I couldn't see the paper and put a puke bucket right outside the gymnasium door (hundreds of students writing at once) in case of emergency. For the true or false section I guessed T (for Terry) every time, and there were at least 40 questions. That's where I must have gotten most of my points, because I honestly couldn't read and comprehend the questions that required written answers. The only thing that weighs on my mind a little is the fact that Dr. Josh Lepawsky was a great professor and must have thought I didn't give a shit about his class. I don't know him well enough to approach him and tell him the story, and chances are he didn't even realize or care that I got such a crappy mark, but I'll toss him a copy of this book when it comes out, and I am sure he'll understand. Stories come first, Doc—anyone can take Geography 101, but not everyone gets to act like a rock star amongst a group of rock stars.

About a week later, Danielle said a package had come for me in the mail. It was a copy of Blue Rodeo's newest album at the time, *The Things We Left Behind*, signed by Jim. It was a vinyl record. I couldn't fuckin' believe he remembered about my collection. There was also a blown-up picture of me in all my glory, standing in the hotel room that night, wearing only my snakeskin cowboy boots, aviator sunglasses, and bikini briefs, singing a song while holding a beer! Jim stayed in touch, met a bunch of my buddies, and we see him a couple of times a year now.

Every spring, in fact, myself, Moondawg, and local musician Chris Ryan, along with J Cud and some of the cast and crew of *Republic of Doyle,* attend a hockey tournament in Toronto called "Exclaim! Hockey Summit of the Arts." The tournament features people involved in the arts industry from all over Canada. Our team has celebrities like Hawco and J Cud, but we also have lesser-knowns like writer Michael Holmes, journalist Tim Wharnsby, and actor Mark O'Brien. Mix in a few ex-hockey pros and regular nine-to-fivers, and there's our team. It is a very fun dressing room to be in, with many different world views. The event promotes fun but is also competitive; there are awards given to the best teams and most non-penalized teams, and each squad is required to do a song/skit afterwards. In 2013, CR and I actually played a few songs (he played guitar, I sang) at the world-famous Horseshoe Tavern, where the Rolling Stones once graced the stage! CR played some of his own stuff, and I closed it out with my version of "Johnny B. Goode" in front of a bunch of rockers. It blew my mind, and is once again something that was made possible through hockey. It's always a great time in Toronto in April, and the event seems to display something I said many times before: musicians and hockey players aren't so different.

Hershey Bears

Even though I didn't play in Hershey for very long—a total of eight games in seven or eight weeks—I enjoyed my time there and am proud to have played for the franchise. The Hershey Bears have been around since the 1930s, making them the oldest team in the American Hockey League. The town is home to the Hershey Company, and chocolate is its claim to fame. It is a tiny place—less than 13,000 people live there—and the proud organization has hosted a record 11 AHL championship parades and seen countless baby-faced prospects develop into bona fide NHL superstars. I am somewhat of a traditionalist when it comes to sports—it is one of the reasons I am so proud to have suited up as a Hab. And as far as the minors go, the Hershey Bears franchise captures the essence of tradition and class. A town that small successfully operating a team for such a remarkable tenure is an achievement. Harrisburg is about 15 kilometres away and makes up much of the fan base, and everyone in the area seems to support their beloved Bears come hell or high water.

When I got the call to go to Hershey, they were the farm team of the Colorado Avalanche (now they're affiliated with the Capitals). But even though I had played three full seasons in the AHL at that point, I wasn't signed by the Avalanche (not every player on an affiliate team has a contract with the big club), so my role was minimal. I was fine with that, and I knew what things would be like going in. The way I saw it, even though I was an AHL veteran, I was a call-up and therefore I knew and accepted my place. I understood they needed me as a fourth-liner, and they had to use their signed prospects more than their free agents in order to develop their skills, and rightly so. I was also just coming back from my latest injury—a forearm laceration that severed tendons, required surgery, and caused permanent damage—and I was still getting used to playing with it. To this day my forearm constantly has pins and needles, and though it feels odd, it doesn't really impede stickhandling or anything. It's just annoying as hell.

My first game was in Albany, and I gave them what they wanted to see early. I went out of my way to hit everything that moved, focusing all of my energy on keeping the puck out of our net and being a sparkplug for the boys. Not long in, Jason Lehoux took exception to the confident spunk I was displaying. He asked me to fight and I happily obliged. (Lehoux is a tough French kid who respectfully had a shot of rum and a beer with me in that small window of time after the post-game showers and before the bus ride.) We had a great tilt, going back and forth for at least half a minute with no clear winner. It was a classic hockey fighter's fight: a lot of punches thrown with little defence. Most of the shots were landed with precision, the fans cheered, we tired ourselves out, the officials came in to break it up, and we gave each other a wink and a pat. We had both done our jobs and were safe for another period. Jason and I had a chat in the sin bin and actually stayed in touch for a period of time outside the game. To be completely honest, he cut me through the lip and I still have a scar on the inside of my mouth for my trouble, but nobody knew it at that moment.

I sucked in and swallowed my blood, and I'll tell you why.

In hockey, blood plays a more important role than you think. Even if they take fighting out of the game, that won't change. (It may even get worse.) If you get a stick in the mouth, for example, and it draws blood, your team gets a five-minute power play, three minutes more than if there is no red stuff. So naturally players show the referee and everyone else at the game the evidence if blood is drawn. When you're in a tilt, though, even if it's a clear draw, the decision goes to the guy who drew blood from his opponent. It sounds primitive, but that's the way it is. After we served our time, I threw some ice cubes into my mouth to water down any hint of crimson on my kisser. I got a few more shifts, potted a lucky assist en route to a victory, and all was good in Albany, New York, that particular night.

I wasn't the only player in the Bears organization who had no secure spot on the team. There were a few of us drifters living at the hotel — and my roomie Steve Parsons was one of them.

Pars is a great fella who deserves a decent description here because he remains a close pal. Sometimes you just meet someone you identify with, and you take something with you from the experience. In my mind, that is one of the main rewards the game of hockey has to offer. Every year a professional hockey player meets, bonds with, and goes to war with new people. The road, though bumpy at times, opens doors and exposes you to new experiences, and inevitably opens your mind in the process. Check out any hockey player's Facebook page. I have all kinds of pals on there I never played one game with, and even more I haven't even played against or spoken to — but when you share experiences like the ones I'm writing about, you establish a common bond. I have had a lot of teammates over the years, and Steve is one of the toughest, kindest, most passionate people I have ever met. Ultimately, he's a kind of walking contradiction.

Pars is a huge man, standing 6-foot-4 and weighing 240 pounds in shape. He can chuck the knuckles with the best of them and also has decent skill, so he isn't a liability on the ice. His hand is bigger than my whole head and he is a very intimidating guy, especially when he's in a bad mood. He is no angel; he's got a quick temper and witty mouth when taunted, but he has a lot of character and is very generous. In May 2012, for example, Pars organized a fundraiser in the small town of Chestermere, Alberta, to raise money and bring awareness to the Alberta Children's Hospital Foundation. He and a bunch of buddies participated in the longest hockey game ever — over 246 hours — and raised over $1.5 million in the process! They didn't do it half-assed either. These guys lived in the rink around the clock and took four-hour shifts on-ice for over 10 days, rarely eating or sleeping. Subjecting your body to this physically gruelling punishment for charity is the epitome of unselfishness. During my two-year Alberta stint in 2007–09, Pars gave me free room and board for three months, and if I thanked him he would get annoyed and change the subject.

One day in Hershey, early in my stay, we were playing the Quebec Citadelles. Pars was our heavyweight — at least two levels ahead of my status in the fighting category. I fought and learned how not to lose too bad if need be, but Pars fought every fight to win, and some guys he regularly beat are still playing in the NHL. He came out of the Canadian college circuit as a professional hockey brawler, which is super-duper rare, and was determined to do anything at all to make it. Since he was a massive specimen, scrapping was a good choice. Anyway, it was my first game playing at home, in Hershey. We had just come back from the road trip to Albany and were excited to play for the home fans, especially me. When we came out for warm-up, I wheeled around the ice without a helmet, hair flowing, aiming all pucks into the upper twining of the net and chewing gum like a rock star. I was scouting the stands for "talent" and wanted to see if any of the boys had good taste in wives. Four or five minutes in, after everyone had stretched, we were getting ready to do some drills, but Pars was standing out by the red line, close to where their team was stretching. He stared directly into their zone. The Quebec guys saw him but didn't say anything. I turned to Bryan Muir, who was also fairly new to the team, and said, "Muirsy, what the fuck is Pars doin' out by the red line?"

"Apparently he does that once in a while," said Muirsy, smirking. "He just comes out and stares at the other team, trying to make eye contact. He may not even touch a puck out here. He is making a point."

"Jesus fucking Christ, Muirsy, who is this fuckin' wing nut? I don't know whether I love him or hate him, but I guess we'll find out."

Pars stayed there for 15 straight minutes and at the end of warm-up he took his gear off and rode the bike hard — after all he still needed to get his legs moving. He said he "had my back" while staring me in the eye like my daddy.

"I can take care of myself, thanks," I said.

You see, from my perspective, Pars saw me as a challenge, and even though we all knew he was tougher, I figured he wanted to make a point. Like a big jungle cat, he was establishing his territory while sending a message to the brass that he was the toughest kid on the block — a macho thing. I went out and fought one of their tough guys, Mathieu Raby. Raby is considerably bigger than me and it was a good-lookin' donnybrook: I was pleased with the outcome and so were my teammates.

After the game, Pars came over and sat down next to me as I iced my hand in the half-stall that was reserved for call-ups like me. (Pars had a real stall from day one on account of his intimidation factor.) I was prepared for some testosterone-filled bullshit comment and was ready to respond when he laughed, "Great job! You really did well there, buddy! Raby's a tough kid. I loved watching you play in junior and I have some relatives in Newfoundland."

I was floored, but like I said, Pars is a walking contradiction and one has to really get to know him before making assumptions.

"Uh, thanks buddy," I said sheepishly, and then he laughed again and strutted towards the shower. By the time I made it in there myself Pars was nearing the end of his wash. He had his eyes closed and he was smiling, letting the water run down his body with his arms spread wide. It reminded me of the movie *The Shawshank Redemption,* when Andy Dufresne (Tim Robbins) successfully digs his way out of prison through miles of walls and sewers and uses the same body language to bask in his happiness at finally emerging in the outside world.

"You know the secret to having good hair?" he said, holding the pose. "It's not washing your hair every day, or even two days. Once, twice a week max. Washing it too much makes it frizzy like that mop you got goin'. Now hurry up, let's go to Shakey's for a beer. We earned it! First one's on me."

With that, Pars left, without a care in the world. If his family and teammates are happy, he's happy. I loved Pars from that moment on. It was his world, and he loved life. He reminded me of myself, but represented the part of me I wanted to be all the time. God knows I can be negative, my moods swing back and forth like a pendulum; I have always thought about things too much. Steve Parsons's attitude towards his whole existence reminded me of that famous old Dale Carnegie quote: "If life deals you lemons, make lemonade." It wasn't that Pars was dealt a shitty hand in life or anything, but whenever something negative happened he had a way of being optimistic and lightening the mood of his pals.

I can see why Pars overcame the odds and made it so far in the hockey world. He worked hard and was permanently optimistic. He was unselfish, respectful, and did what whatever was necessary to get the job done. I quickly realized he wasn't trying to be the alpha male earlier, he was just a good teammate and he was being genuine. He told me over a beer later that evening at Shakey's (a great little dive bar at the time in Hershey that played loud music and served decent grub) that he knew I was wiry and didn't want me to mess with the wrong guy. Pars believed in my abilities more than I did, and told me not to hurt my knuckles any more than I had to.

I had Steve Parsons pegged completely wrong, like many who meet him for the first time. He was protecting my future.

Dallas Maverick

As I mentioned earlier, before I got to Boise in 2001, I attended Dallas Stars training camp. Dale Sullivan — one of my buddies from Calvert, Newfoundland, and nephew of local hockey legend Andy Sullivan — was my roomie down there and this is still one of his favourite tales:

It was early September 2001. Camp was getting intense. There remained around 50 players in Dallas, and I was one of them. Sully hurt his knee pretty bad in one of the exhibition games but tried to play through it and show the Stars brass some spunk. Most guys were already signed by the big team, so in actuality there really weren't many spots being auditioned for. I had a decent camp up to that point. I worked out harder than ever in the summer, as I wanted to prove to the hockey world I could play at the NHL level. I checked into camp with a 7 percent body fat percentage and I scored a 68 percent on the VO2 max test —indicators that I was in great cardiovascular shape. I even attended rookie camp, where I fought bigger, tougher, and scarier John Erskine a handful of times if I fought him once. Hunter Lahache—an extremely tough kid who had 466 PIMs for the Cape Breton Screaming Eagles in the QMJHL the year before—shattered my nose in an intra-squad game on the second day of main camp, but I played through it and scored a goal. I made sure I was at the rink first and I stayed on the ice with one of the coaches—ex-NHLer Bob Bassen—after practice in order to improve. I was a hungry athlete, ready to do whatever it took to win back my reputation as one of the world's best players born in 1977.

Well, this one day we were told to be at the rink at 9 a.m. with workout clothes, but we weren't told why. When we got there, a bus was ready to drive us to our destination, about half an hour outside of town. We arrived and were greeted by a group of people who all seemed to be chipper and suspiciously optimistic about everything; they were led by a fruity-lookin' dude wearing a smile as big as Brian Boucher's five-hole. (I'm not anti-gay. My wonderful uncle Daryl on my dad's side is gay and one of the coolest cats in my family. But this guy looked fruity even on Daryl's terms.) They told us they represented the mental side of sports; we were about to do some "team-building" exercises.

Jesus Christ. I hated this shit. To me, team-building is takin' a punch to the jaw from a heavyweight in order to help your squad get a W. Team-building is passing the biscuit to a player in a slump on an empty net late in a game to get him a goal and boost his confidence. Team-building is blocking a 100-mile-an-hour shot from some hungry sniper in the late stages of the game in order to attain two points and have a guilt-free beer on the bus afterwards. Now, however, we had to listen to some fresh-outta-school jerk-off whose parents paid for his top-tier university degree tell us what we needed to do to become better teammates—and by extension, players. Like I haven't been in the trenches, asshole, gettin' my melon lit up by toughies like Franky Bialowas, Tie Domi, or whatever PIM king was on the other team's menu on any given night, because my team needed a lift. Jesus, it pisses me off just writing this. This dude likely never drew blood for anyone, and probably had never been laid in his life, by the look of him. The first exercise we did was an old classic. Grab a partner, fall backward, partner catches you, and you learn to trust your partner. Did it already in grade three, got the T-shirt. Next drill, please.

We did a few more of these yawners and I figured we were all done. Turns out I was wrong. The set of drills we had done up to this point were just a warm-up. We were told what we'd be doing in the afternoon, and I realized my worst nightmare was about to come true.

I should start by telling you I am terrified of heights. Terrified might even be an understatement. I get dizzy on ladders, I throw up on elevators from time to time, and I am very uneasy on planes. I once dropped out of firefighting school because I couldn't rappel down a building—standard stuff for a firefighter. I threw up in the process. I hate fearing heights, because it's not like I can will myself not to do it. It's a problem that has a mind of its own. I start feeling queasy, and the room goes blurry, and I faint. It has happened so many times, I just don't put myself in that position anymore. Now we had this yam-yam telling us that if we didn't go through the obstacle course laid out in front of us, the team couldn't move on. In order to just begin the test, we needed to strap ourselves into a harness at the top of a fucking light pole.

It's hard for me to explain, but I'll try to make it as clear as I can. There were a set of light poles (I call them light poles because they resembled light poles, but there were no wires or lights attached to them) set up about 60 to 80 feet apart, and they were all attached one way or another. The first was attached to the second by another pole, the second to the third on a tightrope-type thingy, and so on and so on. After the last pole you had to jump in the air and zip-line for around 200 feet, passing the finish line in the process. Piece o' cake right? Well fuck that. I shouldn't do this. I couldn't do this. I wouldn't do this.

Well, wouldn't you know it, the first 40-odd guys finished the course. Many seasoned vets weren't there — they took the morning off — but most of camp's attendees were present. Some looked like they weren't gonna make it but ended up getting through. Some guys acted like they were scared but they were secretly excited — they wanted an easy way to gain brownie points from the brass — including GM Bob Gainey, who was now in attendance. Fan-fucking-tastic.

I kicked and screamed, man. I wanted zero part of this exercise. I knew I couldn't do it. I didn't have the parts. I was unsigned, though, and all of a sudden my character as a player was reduced to scaling a fuckin' light pole and putting on a circus act, so I had to try. Fuck! If I had only known this, I would have numbed the pain with a shot of whiskey or something (that's how I finished the roller coaster in the West Edmonton Mall). I closed my eyes and climbed the pole, yelling general obscenities. I caught the attention of a few of the guys on the ground. I could hear them laughing, which made everything way worse. I had a melting pot of emotions goin' on in my cranium. Pride, fear, revenge, courage, and angst flowed through my veins — racing to see which emotion would win out and take over in this traumatizing time. I was almost at the end of stage one when I made the horrible mistake of looking down.

Immediately mental chaos set in and my brain was on system overload. I blacked out and lunged onto the second pole — the beginning of stage two. I grabbed onto the pole like it was a warm life preserver and I was drowning in the middle of the North Atlantic on a cold day. I realized I was crying uncontrollably. Water flowed from my tear ducts and mixed in with the mucus running from my nose, and I was sucking it in and spitting it out — essentially on everyone down below. I could hear people yelling, "Look at this kid, he's fucking petrified! Ha ha! Guys, get over and see this!" It was my worst nightmare. It wasn't only the heights that were bothering me; my most childish fear was exposed for all to see, as I sat clinging to a light pole, crying and yelling obscenities. I was an example; a man being stripped of his dignity on public display. I just wanted to get down, and I couldn't do it myself. It was at this point that Mr. Bob Gainey — GM and one of my idols and one of the best captains ever to suit up in the NHL — shouted up, attempting to comfort me, "Don't worry, bud, you're safe! It'll be okay."

I looked down with my face so as to be heard clearly, but closed my eyes together with every muscle in my face so my eyes had no way of opening and yelled back down to Mr. Gainey and the crowd, "Oh ya? Well if I'm so safe, why the fuck am I wearing a helmet? Get me the fuck down from here!"

And that was it. A woman came up to rescue me, and had me on the ground before you could say "crybaby." She harnessed me onto her back and talked me through it as she lowered me to the ground and I proceeded to have the most awkward afternoon of my hockey career. It didn't matter how many times I'd fought Erskine, or how many bodychecks I'd doled out in intra-squad games. I was a pussy-on-a-stick for all to witness, and that unforgettable sight is still in many people's heads as if it were yesterday, I'm sure. At this point, the fruity-lookin' dude looked like Clint fucking Eastwood — Dirty Harry version — compared to me.

Looking back, though, two things stand out. 1) Personally I'm glad I actually finished stage one. Only I know in my heart how hard it was, and I'd never be able to do it again unless a loved one's life was in jeopardy. 2) The more I tell that story, the funnier it gets. Back when it happened, I wanted to dig a hole and jump in it, I was so very humiliated. Now, I'm making it public for anyone to see! What a life.

Idaho Steelheads 2001–02

The '01–02 season was pretty much a writeoff from the beginning. I got hurt at the Dallas Stars camp in September, and was injured again on opening night in Boise (a high ankle sprain that would eventually be the reason I had to retire from playing professionally).

Boise is located in the southwest corner of Idaho, and is surrounded by awesome natural scenery highlighted by low-lying mountains that remind me of the foothills outside of Calgary. Danielle's family currently lives right outside of Red Deer with a picturesque view of the Rocky Mountains, and the view from my apartment in Boise was very similar. Rivers and trees are intertwined throughout the comfortably sized city of a little more than 200,000. There are no significant professional sports franchises for hundreds of miles in any direction, so we had a broad fan base and were often the top story in the local sports news (if it was a slow day at Boise State). People seemed to really enjoy the outdoors; all the hiking and fishing that went on reminded me of St. John's—as did the friendly demeanour of the people of Idaho.

My injured ankle nagged at me all year, but I tried to plug through. Still, it meant I played sparingly over the course of the season. I did end up getting into 30 games, and when we lost the final in seven games, I at least felt like a part of the team. Off the ice I would try to do what I could to help out, whether it be volunteer with children's organizations or simply fill water bottles and provide comic relief at the rink. One time, I told the boys I'd figure a way to get us in a positive mood for a road trip we were about to go on, and one of the ways I'd do it was to try to get a letter about our team published in a national magazine. I wrote in to dozens of publications, tried every angle, and then it came to me while we were on the bus playing cards after a few wobbly pops. One of the guys — Jason Cugnet — was reading an issue of *Maxim*, a monthly men's periodical. Cugger was looking at the pictures, of course — they usually depict hot women — but I remembered they had a feedback section in the front that was humour-based. Maybe that was my best shot. Sure enough, I wrote a poem about our upcoming road trip to San Diego, and it got published. For a brief while, fans in other buildings had copies of *Maxim* for me to sign, even though I was sitting on the bench or in the stands most of the year. I tried tracking down the issue for the purposes of this book, but I couldn't find a hard copy anywhere. If anyone wants to, check the "Letters" section of *Maxim*, January or February 2002. I guarantee it's there. We had fun with that one.

By the Skin of My Teeth

I was frustrated a lot that year. My first marriage was failing, my chances of landing a permanent NHL job were dwindling, and to top it all off, parts of my two front teeth were missing. I had lost them in a ball hockey game, representing Newfoundland at a national tournament in Montreal that summer. I could have gone to the hospital right after I lost them, but I wanted to have a few beers with my pals before I left for Dallas the next day. I figured I would just get them done in Texas, forgetting how expensive it would be. The truth of the matter was I was once again only invited to camp, not signed by the Stars, which meant I had to front the whole bill myself. That night I actually drank beer through a straw because the exposed nerves in my teeth hurt so bad, and every day the pain got worse. By the time I got to Boise in late September, it had been two months and I was wearing a mouth guard to get through everyday chores just to prevent the nerves from being exposed. My teeth hurt whenever I breathed in. One of the first things I did when I got to Boise was try to get them fixed, but our trainer warned me the team wouldn't be paying for the dental work, as I got the injury in the summer and wasn't property of Idaho at that point. I was pissed because I had no way out—or so I thought.

I was facing a huge bill and there was nothing I could do about it. My ball hockey insurance only supplied a thousand bones towards the total, which was gonna be at least five grand.

One morning that week I was at the rink early, as usual, and mockingly complained to our doctor. "Doc," I said, "what if I keep these teeth and eventually someone knocks them out worse?" (I looked like Jim Carrey in *Dumb and Dumber*, sporting half teeth). "I mean the chances are I may lose them again if I continue, so maybe I will wait and see."

"Sure," Doc replied. "Of course we'd fix them up nice. And knowing how injury-prone you are, it may actually happen," he laughed, never suspecting I was already devising a plan. I waited until after practice and called a few pals over to tell them the news of my scheme. Some laughed, some grimaced, some stood in disbelief, and at the end of the day, bets were being placed about whether I'd follow through . . .

The pressure was on.

It's as vivid in my memory as the day I saw my first stripper as a

13-year-old with a face full of pepper. I waited three weeks so as not to be obvious, and I told the boys in our morning skate it was time to put my plan in action. Most of us lived in the same apartment complex, so all the boys were there that night, waiting to see if I really was stupid enough to do it. I was about to knock my own teeth out, with a hammer.

I waited until after my nap, which always came immediately after practice, and grabbed a half dozen beers out of Kris Graf's fridge. I popped in a VHS tape of *The Simpsons* to lighten my mood. Once I finished my sixth pop, I borrowed a small toy hammer from one of the neighbour's kids—it was metal but tiny and seemed as though it may be able to chip off some of my teeth. I walked over to the bathroom mirror and figured I would lightly tap my teeth, they would chip a little and I would say I did it in a practice. Then I would be home free . . .

I started whacking my teeth with the toy, but they weren't budging. After several blows, I figured it was time to use a bigger tool. I went downstairs, and told my teammate and close friend Bobby Stewart he was a big tool himself and asked him to find me something worth using.

Stewy found me a small sledgehammer.

Back in my place, I realized I had better be accurate: the end of the thing was large and rounded so there was only a small margin for error. Plus I was half lit. "Fuck it," I said, and I swung away and . . . I pulled up short at the last second, splitting my lip in two so bad that my tongue could go right through it. I was leaking now, and I had to finish the job.

The next swing drove my head so hard that I knocked out all four front teeth into the sink. The mess was large, the moment surreal, and my buddies watched in bewilderment. All I remember from that point on was laughter. We had a few beers in celebration. I knew my task was only partway finished though; I had to hide the evidence until I got onto the ice.

The next day at the rink was a challenge, but I got through it. I even spoke with the doctor and trainer. I was around the corner doing up my skates and they were in the training room as usual. They would remember talking to me, but hadn't actually seen me. Self-mutilation didn't even surface in their minds, I am sure. I taped my teeth to my skin under my jersey, and when I finally hit the ice I told Stewy to grab a puck and whiz it by my ears as I skated around the net. I acted like I slipped on a puck trying to avoid his errant shot and threw the teeth across the ice. I nicked over my gums as to produce some blood, and ran back into the room in what appeared to be agony. The doc couldn't believe his eyes and confirmed I must be the most unlucky hockey player he'd come across in a long time.

Seven grand later, I had a brand new set of Chiclets, baby!

What's All the Buzz About?

Sometimes people ask me about drugs and hockey. I am being totally honest when I say I never saw anyone do steroids; I almost never heard anyone talk about doing them. I assume people were experimenting, as in any sport. But there couldn't have been that many. One fella—I won't mention his name—came to camp chubby one year and told us he did 'roids. He was junior-aged and as big as a bear. He hadn't worked out during the summer, he said; instead, he boozed and barbecued, leaving it to the 'roids to make him bigger! Another guy I played with in Fredericton—Dave Morissette—admitted to taking steroids during his career in a book he wrote a few years back called *Mémoires d'un dur à cuire* (*Memoirs of an Enforcer*), and although I was unaware of it at the time, the revelation didn't surprise me. He was the most intimidating physical specimen I have ever played with. I saw him put Bobby Probert out of a game after cutting him over the eye with a massive right to the orbital bone. "Moose," as he was called, was a genuinely nice guy. I'd go to bat for him any day. I guess he felt pressured to always be at the top of his game, and even though I never went down that road myself, I can see where he was coming from. It's not easy to be a tough guy—it's one of the hardest and most unique jobs in all of sports. The guys who do it aren't looking for an easy way out when they juice; they want to be the best they can be in order to provide for their families. Still, I take no pity on people who get busted—they know the rules.

I think the reasons for getting involved with performance-enhancing drugs are different for each individual athlete. Barry Bonds for example, was already an all-star player and future Hall of Famer before he apparently decided to take 'roids and smashed baseball's coveted single-season home run record (73 in 2001), eventually edging Hank Aaron's career benchmark of 755 by finishing with 762 in 2007. They caught him, but they caught a lot of dudes that excelled during that era of baseball. The thing is, Bonds won't admit he consciously juiced. Same thing with the A-Rod situation in 2013. These guys are so proud, they don't want to admit their flaws, even though it's the humble path to take and they'd get more respect. I see a certain level of greed there: a superior athlete changing the face of the game and accepting all the accolades that go along with it, but not admitting the truth when it came time to fess up. Other guys, like New York Yankee Andy Pettitte, admitted they were wrong and moved on. I can easily forgive that and understand where Pettitte was coming from, trying to keep up with the Joneses and extend his career. In Moose's case, though, he was trying to save a minor league job which paid him five figures a year and maybe catch a few games up top (which he did late in his career—11 games played from 1998 to 2000 with the Habs).

I didn't do much more than drink when I played, for a number of reasons.

One road trip when I played in Boise stands out. We played on a Monday night in Bakersfield, Tuesday and Wednesday we were off, and then we were in San Diego on the Thursday. Our place in San Diego was cheap for the area — West Coast Hockey League budgets were far from the big time — but I thought it was still a fantastic set-up. It had a distinctly Californian feel: small cactuses here and there, an unintentionally cool addition to the small half-kept flower beds found throughout the hotel grounds. You could get into the rooms from the outside, and on the way tiny lizards ran amok. Tumbleweed was plentiful, and there was a small but swimmable outdoor pool. The water wasn't overly clean, but it wasn't mud, and we didn't give a shit. We could drink, gawk at the scenery walking by, and save money before hitting the bar with a $20 bill. (I remember winning a bet with Jeremy "Lazy-eye" Mylymok over whether or not a passerby's tits were real. He said yes. I leapt out of the pool and ran across the street to ask her, and she admitted they were fake and brand new. Mylsy still owes me 50 bones for that, come to think of it.)

That Tuesday was like Christmas, because we had a green light to get shit-faced with no game the next day, and we were in San Diego! Our coach, John Olver, ran a pretty tight ship, but he was cool with us staying out until the bars closed this particular night, as long as we were at practice and ready to go for 10:30 the next morning. We were on a winning streak.

In the morning a few of us — Jeremy Yablonski, Scotty Burt (my old roomie in Red Deer), and Kris Graf went to Tijuana. Being only a half hour away by cab, it cost us something like 20 bucks each. Myself and Yabbo got lost and went on this crazy tour around the city with some shifty-lookin' locals, and we could smell trouble brewing.

Literally, we could smell weed unlike any I had ever smelled. I took a hit of this one badass dude's joint when he passed it around, and that was it, I was completely fucked. I had smoked pot a handful of times before and I didn't mind it, but I hated the paranoia that sometimes came with the high.

Within seconds I was gigglin' and I couldn't stop, even though part of me was paranoid. After all, we were on the backstreets of Tijuana —touristy-lookin' gringos ripe for the pickin'—and these guys were all staring and laughing. Yabbo said to trust him, we were okay, he hadn't smoked any weed and was in control of the situation. This just made matters worse: I started thinking these guys had a plan to fuck with my brain and who knows what else. At least if Yabbo had done it I would have someone who understood how stoned I was. Next thing you know, I started running for my life. I went like Forrest Gump for 10 minutes, until I couldn't run anymore. When I turned around I realized how funny I must have looked.

Some of the guys from the team who came to Tijuana after us were in a taxi with no doors, gliding behind me. They said me and Yabbo were only like 50 feet away at all times—they watched us from the deck of the restaurant they had stopped to eat at. The "badass" Mexicans were doing construction on a site close by and had come out for a joint and glass of ice water because they were sweating to death inside. I had been stereotyping all of them in my haze. When we returned to the restaurant I ate half a dozen tacos and had a great chat with the construction workers. I told them I was sorry for acting like a bigot fool and happily they accepted my apology. We left them tickets for Thursday night and tossed a few pucks at them in warm-up. Good guys. And as good as a reason as any to not do drugs, kids! I believe weed should be legal, for many reasons, but I still don't advocate smoking it when you're a young hockey player. It slows you down.

Later that day when we got back to our rooms, the desk clerk told us there was a concert that evening at the arena. I decided to jet over to the concert last minute and check it out. When I got there I was still in a great mood, and I ended up smoking some more Mary-Jane again with a random stranger. Here's the journal entry I wrote when I got back to the hotel:

San Diego, 2001

"Clapton rocks! Clapton rocks!" The crowd at San Diego Arena was going wild, chanting for their hero . . . to finally take the stage after what seemed like an eternity of "Project Death," the mediocre cover band that weren't advertised on the concert ticket but had just opened for the aging guitar legend. These guys seemed to be nothing more than a few local dudes living the dream, and this appeared to be the band's peak, playing in front of 13,000 or 14,000 . . . They did however seem to be having fun for a moment, serenading the crowd with a set that included Quiet Riot, Iron Maiden, and Judas Priest covers and a handful of originals that, frankly, nobody cared to hear . . .

I had always wanted to see Eric Clapton in concert, ever since I was a young boy growing up Newfoundland. My parents, Gail and Terry Ryan, Senior, had lived in the United States for most of the 1970s, my mom following my father as he tried to live his hockey dream and make it to the big leagues . . . My dad's biggest passion was music, so wherever he went, he could be found at the local record shops perusing the latest must-have vinyl records and rock tees, and checking out live acts; rock stars like the Rolling Stones, up and comers like Bruce Springsteen, "has-beens" like Herman's Hermits, and legends like Elvis Presley. I grew up listening to all the music my parents collected along the way—which amounted to thousands of albums—and my single favourite artist was Eric Clapton. He had so much raw talent, and the simplicity of his live shows accentuated his talent and intensified the music . . . The music was the thrill. I was born in 1977, and all through the 1980s I made it a point: someday I would see the man live in concert.

Fast forward to 2001, and here we are. I finally had my chance to see "Slowhand" here in San Diego. I could feel my palms sweating and was extremely anxious for this concert to begin. Ironically, I was now in the middle of my own minor league hockey journey, and I was playing for the Idaho Steelheads of the West Coast Hockey League—a league far removed from the glitz and glamour of the NHL . . . Our first road trip of the 2001–02 season was what the other players referred to as The California Swing, where we were set to play the San Diego Gulls, Long Beach Ice Dogs, and Bakersfield Condors. Tonight though, it was all about the single most anticipated moment of my youth—watching Eric Clapton live in concert.

The stadium was old, but it held around 15,000 and had a distinct "feel." A lot of these new corporate arenas are built to satisfy the needs of the elite. The luxury boxes are equipped with everything from booze to big screen televisions, making the transition from the daytime ivory towers these silver-spooners tend to work in as comfortable as possible. The acoustics in places like this are generally not good, as they are usually built for CEOs and celebrities and tailor-made for the purposes of the local NBA or NHL team. The San Diego Arena was old school though—there were no luxury boxes at all and the fans were crammed into every section like sardines. The arena dates back to the 1950s and reveals its age in various ways, from the outdated concert photos lining the corridors (Frank Sinatra, Jimi Hendrix, Liza Minnelli) to the No Smoking signs painted on the walls, which were only necessary in a time where you could still spark up a cigarette in many public venues without breaking the law. The seats in the San Diego Arena were of the bucket style and made mostly of pine, reminding one of how many generations have been entertained in the building and how broad a spectrum of entertainers must have performed in it over the years.

Even the concession stand was unique. The menu included sugary treats, seafood, tacos, burgers . . . and everything in between. This gave the building a smell I will honestly never forget. The scent upon entering was dominated by cotton candy and wood, and was actually a welcome change from the normalness of regular venues. The security workers and ushers (male and female) wore tight red three-piece suits with bright white collared shirts and big black bow ties. On their heads, they wore black top hats with a red ribbon and their charcoal black shoes were so shiny I am sure you could see your reflection in them. The entire ensemble looked classy, amusing, and clean all at once. It triggered memories I had of my childhood bedtime, when my grandfather Bill would fill my imagination with stories of going to the theatre in the 1930s and '40s. Being in the San Diego Arena, in a word, felt comfortable.

I went to the concert with six or seven friends, and we had decent seats. I, however, traded my ticket and paid $200 extra for one in the front row. The front row is a strange place, especially at a concert. In a hockey game, there is glass separating the crowd and the players, but at a concert, the front row is filled with hooligans, superfans, and stalkers, so it has a feeling entirely different from any other section in the arena. I remember looking to my right and seeing a big, burly, trucker-looking dude wearing excess denim, reeking of B.O., and sporting a large face tattoo of a spider's web. To my left sat a young girl with green hair, multiple piercings, and shockingly white skin which also featured tattoos, the most notable being the word "Roxy" scrawled across her bosom in block letters . . . She was energetic and excited to see the show, offering everyone what she described as "the best MaryJane in Cali," and passing around a bottle of Jack Daniel's for good measure. Roxy *was sitting in front of a group of bikers wearing Harley-Davidson attire from head to foot, which explains why nobody was giving her a hard time for carrying the drugs and alcohol. These guys were behind me to my left, and gave me more of a sense of protection than conflict.*

As I continued to take in all the sights and sounds around me in what seemed like a dream at this point, the lights in the stadium went out. One light shone down from the top of the stage and was pointed at the lone microphone that stood in the middle looking naked. Up to this point I hadn't even noticed the mic, but now it was on display, which meant only one thing . . . it was time for Eric Clapton!

What happened next is carved into my memory, as much a part of my mental being as the tattoos I carved on my arms are part of my physical self. Eric Clapton . . . my hero, walked slowly onto the stage, exactly how I pictured. He was dressed in a plain white T-shirt and raggedy blue jeans, with plain black military-style boots and a scruffy look. His hair was light brown in colour with hints of grey and brought attention to Clapton's age and wisdom. The look was plain, and symbolized the emphasis of the music. No special effects. As good ol' Slowhand approached the mic, he looked up, not saying a word, and looked me straight in the eyes for a millisecond. Even though the moment didn't last long, it seemed to me like Clapton knew I was coming and why I was there. He ripped into "Layla"—my favourite Clapton offering—kicking off a musical extravaganza that I will never forget. Goosebumps littered my body, and tears of joy and awe streamed down my face as I reminisced about growing up in Mount Pearl and all the time I had spent listening to the rock legend that stood before me. I was the luckiest man on earth. I looked at Roxy, took a hit of her joint and swig of her JD, and leaned on the stage, proceeding to experience what will no doubt always remain one of the single best moments of my life.

Cincinnati/Orlando

2002–03

Playing for the Cincinnati Cyclones, I was having a hard time dealing with the idea of retirement. I knew my career was ending; the more we played, the more I hurt. Practices were excruciating. Before games I had to have my ankle frozen — and for a while, at least, I couldn't feel anything. For those who think I'm exaggerating, I am not. It's exactly what it sounds like, and it's fairly common. The doc would freeze the general area of a player's injury by injecting an anesthetic, and for three or four hours the affected area would feel as good as new . . . But then the game ended, and the freezing wore off — usually when you were driving home.

It was about a half an hour's commute to my apartment complex from downtown Cinci, where our 15,000 seat arena was located (right next to the home of the Reds and Bengals), and my ankle would be stiff and painful by the time I got home. If I went out for beers with the boys, the pain was numbed a little due to the fantastic masking effects of booze, but it always felt even worse in the mornings when I chose this kind of self-medication, because of the dehydration that results from drinking alcohol. With guys like Robin "Corzy" Delacour and Steve "Ace" Gallace—who could tip 'em back as productively as anyone I had come across in the game—one always led to two, which led to a two-four. My productive playing options were limited and I knew it. The biggest problem was the tough schedule of pro hockey: at least 70 or 80 games of intense physical punishment and sacrifice. My body wasn't capable of that: I was going to have to call it a career.

Hurt So Good

One shitty morning, after I called Malcolm Cameron and told him I was hangin' 'em up, myself and Corzy went for breakfast and shot the shit over a coffee and a bite. We'd done this on many occasions, and browsed the Ohio concert listings. Music always makes me feel better when I am down, and as luck would have it one of my favourite artists ever—John Mellencamp—was playing in Dayton the next night. It was just what the doctor ordered; I figured the concert would be sold out, so I decided to make a day of it and check out Dayton before the author of such classic heartland tunes as "Jack & Diane" and "Rain on the Scarecrow" put on a show for me and 7,000 others. The only problem was that I didn't have a ticket, but I was willing to pay a little extra if I had to in order to see the man formerly known as John Cougar.

I admired the way he wrote, sang, and performed his own music—songs that always seemed injected with the kind of Americana that the average middle-class person could identify with. My musical opinion may not matter to many folks, but I love artists that are multi-dimensional. Next to Jessica Simpson, Ke$ha, or Katy Perry, singer-songwriters and classic rockers reign as superior musicians, even when their album sales don't show it. The others are just performers. Like the Buggles said in 1979, "Video Killed the Radio Star."

When I got to the concert venue, I stood in line to buy one of the few nosebleed tickets that remained, and I saw a very familiar face moseying up the stairs to gate five. It was Paul O'Neill, baseball legend and sports icon. O'Neill was known for his character, and for winning five World Series titles and making five all-star game appearances while playing for the Cincinnati Reds and New York Yankees. My dad was always a Yankees fanatic and I became one too, by extension. T. Ryan, Senior, was a great ball player—as a 15-year-old he was selected to the national all-star team—and cheered for the Yanks because of their rich history. We were Habs fans for the same reason. I knew more about Babe Ruth as a preschooler then I did about *Sesame Street*'s Big Bird or Oscar the Grouch. The man they call "the Babe"—George Herman Ruth—was, in my dad's words, "The best player to ever play the game." For Dad, the 1980s were all about Don Mattingly, and in the 1990s Paul O'Neill was the ballplayer my father wanted me to take after in my summertime game of choice. Sports, for Dad, were always, always about team, team, team . . . I am the same way with my son Ty: I too make a team-first attitude a mantra.

As the legend himself, Paul O'Neill, walked by, I jumped out of line and introduced myself. Half cut from an amazing tailgate party being hosted by some locals, I stumbled and stuttered like a giddy schoolgirl caught in a stare-down with Justin Bieber under a moonlit waterfall. I asked him for an autograph, told him I was a big fan, and backed it up with some above-average knowledge of his career and the great game itself. As I stood there looking like a deer caught in Mr. O'Neill's headlights, a fan of the Cyclones happened to be walking in and said, "Hey Terry, good game the other night." Mr. O'Neill then asked me who I was, and I told him I was a minor league hockey suitcase, currently playing for the Cincinnati Cyclones an hour's drive away. I told him I once had a cup of coffee with the Montreal Canadiens on hockey's biggest stage. With that, Paul laughed and said he had taken his kids to a few Cyclones games. I am sure he didn't know who I was, but he acted like he did and invited me into the luxury box he was using that night anyway. It was a kind of mutual respect, pro-athlete style.

Flabbergasted by the series of events that had taken place that day, I accepted the offer and watched the first four songs of the Mellencamp with one of the most respected names ever to be mentioned at my parents' place back on Park Avenue. I didn't want to wear out my welcome, and I could tell that Paul was being a nice guy and humouring me, so I took the hint and moved on to a seat behind the stage. I wasn't even able to see Johnny M. perform, and listened to muffled lyrics from behind the speakers.

That's when I broke down and cried like a baby, frustrated at my attitude. I couldn't help but feel selfish. There I was, depressed that my ice hockey professional career was coming to an end. I was feeling sorry for myself, tripping over my bottom lip over the fact I was about to hear the term "first-round bust" a few tens of thousands of times. And then it hit me like a ton of bricks: despite everything, I was one lucky motherfucker. I mean, how many folks had these kinds of experiences so frequently?

I think I improved as a person that day. (A cheesy sentence, I know, but it's true.) In a sense, it was how I began to accept my fate in the hockey world. On the drive back to Cinci, for the first time, I really thought about life after hockey. I tried to add up all the crazy experiences I'd had over the years, and over the next few months I dug out all my journals. Someday, I figured I would share my tales with the rest of the world and maybe try to show other people how fortunate hockey players can be. I was a First Round Nothing, and proud of it.

The Cincinnati ownership group included one of the purest goal scorers in the history of hockey, Phil Esposito, and Academy Award–winning actor Cuba Gooding, Jr. I am not sure who was responsible, but for training camp we toured parts of Austria, Germany, and Italy and played exhibition games against professional teams in places like Innsbruck, Munich, and Milan. It was a great experience—one of the best road trips ever—and I know all the boys appreciated it. We had free travel on a European tour, and lots of guys who didn't end up making the team got to come along and were treated like gold.

Our coach, Malcolm Cameron, got a little upset in Munich when we hit Oktoberfest for the afternoon and came back to the bus at 10 bells loaded drunk, full of nothing but beer and sausages. The boys were loud and out of hand, and the smell was putrid. Looking back, I am glad we did what we did (not a lot of people get to be in the heart of Germany for its most famous celebration), but I totally see where Malcolm was coming from. He was a well-organized new coach with high hopes. He had a university hockey career largely due to sheer determination and work ethic and didn't want to lose his job to some veteran of one of hockey's higher stages because of our irresponsibility.

Malcs also wasn't happy in Vienna when Corzy and I fought in warm-up in order to scare the opposing team (we were trying to look crazy and therefore intimidating). Espo smirked but was also dumbfounded. We did it for a joke; dropped our gloves in the middle of doing the horseshoe drill in pre-game skate. I told Espo I was carrying some angst from the famous '72 series he starred in (and in my opinion one of the top five moments in our nation's history, for reasons that go far beyond hockey). We all laughed about it on the way home, though, and I still keep in contact with many of those guys due to the bonds we forged on that trip. And then, 12 games into the season, my ankle essentially gave out on me.

Fun in the Sun

In early December, I signed my retirement papers and drove back to the Rock. Normally I'd have the music cranked. But as I was driving through New York, gazing at the Statue of Liberty, I realized I hadn't even put the stereo on. I had been daydreaming about virtually every aspect of my life. My first marriage was about to end and my pro hockey career was over, and there was an emptiness that came with my newfound acceptance of the position I was in. Since the Mellencamp concert I understood my fate, but it still seemed sad. I felt I had so much more to give, but my body just wouldn't work well enough to deliver for my coaches and teammates—and that sucked.

When I got to Newfoundland, I had to find a job; my options were limited. I remember hearing the words "stay in school, kids" from my elementary teachers and realized I should have at least taken more courses while playing and living the good life. A few years earlier, I'd been making great money in my profession's top league, and now I needed to get a construction gig or work in the mill. Remember the line from *Slap Shot*? "Chrysler plant, here I come!" Well, that would have been awesome, considering my situation.

By Christmas 2002, I had only been off skates five weeks, but I had already put on 20 pounds of pure fat. Drinking too much and eating like a pig had the boys at home calling me "Terry Rhinoceros." In February, I tipped the scales at 235—a full 35 pounds heavier than I was when I reported to training camp in September. I love to eat, and when I live a sedentary lifestyle I gain weight rapidly. All the same, my phone kept ringing. Various minor league teams were wondering if I was interested in playing: it was playoff push time and it never hurts to add some experience and depth, especially in the minor leagues, because signed players can be called up and unsigned players can sign a deal with another team and leave.

One night I returned from the Rob Roy and checked my messages. (The Rob Roy is a fixture of George Street now owned by my good pal Kevin English. Kevin comes from the most successful basketball family ever in Newfoundland. His brother Carl English is a legend: he was a college star with University of Hawaii, has played for Team Canada numerous times since 2000, and currently plays professional basketball in Spain.) "Hey T Bone, it's Zac Boyer here. We have an opening in Orlando, I have a concussion, and we need a veteran. I am going to become an assistant coach for the rest of the year. Our head coach is Stan Drulia—great guy. I heard you're a fat pig right now, so shed whatever weight you can in a week and get down to O-Town. I knew you always wanted to win a ring, and here's your chance. One last kick at it, buddy. We are in first place, and in case you didn't hear me, we play in Orlando, Florida!"

Zac and I had been teammates in Colorado Springs a couple of years before, and we got along great. I looked up to him, as I look up to all the members of the Kamloops WHL organization. He scored the biggest goal in Blazers history, netting the winner of the Memorial Cup final on a nifty feed from Scott Niedermayer in 1992, which led to the Blazers winning their third Mem Cup championship in four years in 1995.

They are simply one of the best junior hockey teams ever. The Memorial Cup is one of the hardest trophies to win, not only because you have to beat the best teams in all three branches of Canadian major junior hockey—the Western Hockey League, the Ontario Hockey League, and the Quebec Major Junior Hockey League—but because at most you have only five years to do it, and the vast majority of junior hockey players only play three, between the ages of 17 and 19. The Blazers of the early to mid-1990s were incredible and produced players like Scott Niedermayer, Darryl Sydor, Corey Hirsch, Nolan Baumgartner, Shane Doan, Jarome Iginla, Tyson Nash, Jason Strudwick, Brad Lukowich, Darcy Tucker, Ryan Huska, Hnat Domenichelli, Steve Passmore, Jason Holland, and Chris Murray. These are just some of the guys who starred for K-Town and played some significant NHL games. Others, like Randy Petruk, Aaron Keller, Zac, Craig Lyons, and "Rocket" Rod Stevens were superstar juniors who, for one reason or another, never made it to the bigs, but given the right break would have not only fit in but been impact guys. The team's fans—whether at Riverside Coliseum or the Kamloops Memorial Arena, where the Blazers played home games prior to 1992—are plentiful and loud, and love their hometown heroes. I thought it was the model junior franchise.

Without explaining every detail of the next week—well, let's just say I had an itch that needed scratching, and I was soon on the plane to Orlando.

When I arrived in Florida I knew I had made the right decision. The league was the now defunct Atlantic Coast Hockey League; the hockey was okay, but at a lower level than any I had played at before. I would liken it to Single A-level baseball. There were some grizzled free agent vets like Chris LiPuma and David Goverde, and there were guys fresh out of junior getting their first taste of pro. We all realized we weren't getting to the Show, but there was a quiet understanding amongst us that we were lucky to be treated like NHLers in a major city like Orlando. Our owner, David Waronker, was a hip young businessman in his early 40s — an approachable, accommodating individual. My ankle was painful and I was eating like a rabbit, so at first I experienced frequent dizziness. A few beers in the hot Florida sun on top of my lettuce and dressing diet meant I was tits up in a hurry. I held off any boozin' with the boys until I started playing games — I figured I'd drink out of the trophy if we won. The team was in first place by a landslide, and I was told I could start playing when I felt comfortable, so the pressure was minimal.

Kevin Costin, our trainer, shot my ankle full of a heavy dose of cortisone, which basically numbed it for a month. I started playing and the team kept dominating. I played the last nine games of the season and then the playoffs, and we breezed through undefeated. I think they would have won without me, but it felt good to contribute and finally get a championship ring (Mr. Waronker spoiled us with Stanley Cup–style finger-pieces), which I still wear to this day. It was bittersweet for me, because I led our team in playoff goal scoring and even earned a few invites to NHL camps, but realistically I knew that was it and respectfully declined.

About two weeks after the season, the cortisone wore off and I couldn't even walk normally. Cortisone only hides pain. The extra damage I had done by playing for not even two months made my ankle feel worse than the day I injured it, but I didn't care. I felt a kind of vindication in winning my last game as a pro, regardless of what league it was. I remember LiPuma (who had won a few championships himself, and who also had a cup of coffee in the Show) telling me that I would always vividly remember every last player from a championship team. And he was right — we had some beauties.

My best pal from that team was Ryan Anderson, a tall, skinny kid from Bowsman, Manitoba, who had no business playing eight years as a pro on talent alone. But he was so good at harnessing team chemistry that he got in more than 500 games, splitting his time between the Austin Ice Bats and the Orlando Seals. On the ice he'd never had a 10-goal season, but he hit the 200-PIM level six times. We were cut from the same cloth as far as personality goes and found comedy in everything. After the big win against Knoxville in the finals, he skated around the ice completely naked, drinking beer with a big grin on his face. When we arrived back in Orlando we both put on Daisy Duke shorts, snakeskin cowboy boots, and duck-hunting jackets, before hitting the town shit-faced. I have only met a few guys who have my lack of inhibition when it comes to that stuff, and "Skinny," as we called him, had more crazy in his pinky finger than I had in my whole body. When I spoke with him in April 2012, he was just home from a Skrillex concert—which he attended wearing a Speedo and a lifeguard's whistle, nothing else.

That summer, I was selected for the Canadian national ball hockey team by George Gortsos, the coach, and Tony Iannitto, the GM. (For some reason my ankle hurts far less in a sneaker than a skate.) I had always played ball hockey—it is a very popular sport in Newfoundland—but I was overweight, so my playing time was limited. I was still around 220 pounds, which was too heavy for me to perform at my best.

When I got to Sierre, Switzerland, for the worlds, I knew I wouldn't play much, so I did what I could to help the team off the floor. I played on the fourth line with Ray Callari and Dennis Bettencourt—two beauties who played their roles well. I filled water bottles, took charge of the music in the room, and made sure the boys were always in good spirits. I was a rookie again, and humbled even to be part of the team. I did dress for every game, and even got out for a few shifts in the final against the Czech Republic—a 6–1 victory (according to Coach G, "the best ball hockey game Canada ever played"). I was elated. Three months earlier, I hadn't ever won a championship, and now I had two under my belt, this one a world title. With Skinny's antics fresh in my mind, I stripped down and did a lap of the arena with my birthday suit on. What a fantastic feeling! Alexandre Burrows, who went on to become an NHL star with the Vancouver Canucks, was outstanding for us, winning the tournament scoring title and solidifying his status as the world's best player. He played in the ECHL that year, but persevered and soon enough hit the big time.

When we got to the hotel after the game, we watched a terrible feed of game seven of the Stanley Cup final, which ended up being one of the most-watched television events of the decade back home, as Ray Bourque won his elusive Stanley Cup with Colorado in the seventh game of the finals, after spending almost his entire Hall of Fame career with the Boston Bruins. Don Cherry and Ron MacLean were chatting on the CBC after the game, and to my surprise — hell, to everyone's surprise — they opened by congratulating me on my championship with the Orlando Seals a couple of months before. This was a surreal feeling — Grapes always treated me well, and Ron MacLean is to this day a good pal, but I never expected the mention on *Hockey Night in Canada*. It remains one of the best days of my life.

Even though my two championships were not exactly on the general public's radar, Grapes and Ronny Mac gave my situation some legitimacy by announcing my retirement to all of Canada. They actually knew about my season, and I was blown away. These are two of the nicest, most sincere gentlemen you will ever meet. Some people may not always agree with their politics or what they say, but I urge those folks to think about this: the public sees them chat for less than a half hour a week. They don't get to see that they're well rounded, charitable individuals and that there is a lot more depth to their personalities than people think! Grapes is more controversial, of course, but Ron can be fixed on viewpoints that aren't always the most popular as well. He's one of the smartest people I know. Ron and I continued to hang out in PEI at Brad Richards's golf tournament every summer, and even today I drop him a line here and there. If I mentioned all the ways Ron and Don have impressed me with acts of good Samaritanism, I'd be writing a hundred more pages. Take it from me, the boys are alright.

Ball hockey may not be a mainstream sport, but it's a great game and it's growing. Newfoundland has a long history in the sport, and after playing for Team Canada I decided I'd never disrespect all the legends of the game from my own province by reporting out of shape again. Once I worked myself back into tip-top shape—on a Newfoundland reality TV show called *Define Yourself*, developed in part, as luck would have it, by my pal Mike O'Neil—I dedicated myself to being as good at ball hockey as I could be. It felt like a second chance of sorts. Mike is an ex-teammate and family friend and asked me to be on his program because he knew he could help me, and I'll never forget that. By 2013 I was one of the captains of the national squad, had won two world championships and two national titles (in 2010 our team, the Newfoundland Black Horse, won gold at the national championships we hosted, becoming the first team from Newfoundland in over 20 years to accomplish the feat), and had travelled all over the world as a result of some key people having confidence in me. I give full credit to George Gortsos and Tony Iannitto for believing in me. If I had met those guys a little earlier, maybe things would have turned out differently on the ice, but don't mistake my curiosity for regret. I am proud of my place in the ball hockey community—once you win a world championship (I don't care what the sport is), the people you do it with are family.

The Last Decade

Knights for Life

In August 2002, the National Ball Hockey Championships were held in St. John's. Growing up, the sports I played were baseball, hockey, ball hockey, and soccer, and I was fortunate enough to go to top-level national championships in all four at different points.

In most sports, Newfoundland was typically ranked with the sporting powerhouses of the Yukon, Northwest Territories, and PEI—we had as much chance of winning as Liberace did of picking up a biker chick in some Texas dive while listening to Mötley Crüe. It didn't happen. There were, however, a few sports where we had a shot at gold— rugby, curling, and fast-pitch softball come to mind—and ball hockey was one of them. Local legends like Dick French, Tommy "One-Eye" Christopher, Andy Sullivan, and Gerry "Fats" Noftall were idols when I was a young lad with a pocketful of Popeye Cigarettes and Big League Chew on the bustling streets of Mount Pearl.

Our scrappy squad made it to the semis, and we were set to play against the rough and tumble Montreal Black Knights. The game was in my hometown, Mount Pearl, because the tourney's main venue, the newly built Mile One Centre in St. John's, was being used for the other semi-final.

The Montreal team had some tough customers from tough backgrounds, and for the most part their guys were of Italian descent. They hung out together and stayed separate from the other teams, opting to eat on their own and get their own accommodations, far away from the local hotel where everyone else stayed. They looked, acted, and sounded like members of the mafia, and most teams stayed away from mixing it up physically or verbally with these dudes.

This, of course, made no sense to me.

The stage was set: Newfoundland versus Quebec in the semis of my first big ball hockey tournament. The Mount Pearl crowd was fired up — and my retired minor hockey jersey hung in the rafters.

We didn't disappoint. The Knights were a top-ranked team and had played together for a few years. We were a hard-working bunch, thrown together so that there would be a competitive host squad. After the first, the score was knotted up at one. They were outshooting us, but not by a landslide, and our goalie, Brian "the Wall" Abbott, was playing well. The Knights scored on the power play early in the second to pull ahead, and we had to go for it: there are only two periods in ball hockey.

For those of you expecting a predictable David-and-Goliath-type finish to this tale, think again.

We beat the net down and threw everything we could at them. I missed on a breakaway that would have sent the crowd into a frenzy if I'd put it in, and they scored on the ensuing rush with about four minutes remaining, making the score 3–1. The game wasn't technically over, but these guys were too good to blow that kind of lead, and we knew it. The missed opportunity stuck in my head, and I was pissed off, big time. My blood was boiling, and the trash-talking—which had been going on all game—was turned up a notch.

With two minutes left in the game — and our season — I walked by their bench and they gave me an earful. "First-round bust" and "Give the money you stole back to the Habs" and "*Tu es con, Terry Ryan, va te faire foutre!*" were three favourites that day. I snapped back with "I hope you enjoyed paying to watch me play, boys, thanks for helping pay my salary," and a few other well-practised comebacks.

During this exchange of verbal vomit, I lost it. The Habs situation, losing in my hometown, missing the breakaway, and the Montrealers' persistent bullshit fired me up. It was go time.

"Hey guys, go win your trophy and jerk each other off. See if I give a fuck. I am better at ice hockey anyway—where they pay players. I made more money in a day than you will all year, you chickenshit wops . . ."

This struck a chord, as you would expect. It was a personal attack against their team and race. I would like to point out that I never made close to the amount of money I referred to—I was just trying to stir the pot. And I love the culture and have nothing against Italians. But I go for the jugular when I'm pissed (I think this is what happens most of the time when guys get caught using racial slurs). Something had to give.

The Montreal player closest to where I was standing punched me in the nose. I wiggled my mitts—hockey's universal invitation to dance with your fists. I could hear my teammate Curtis Baggs yelling for me to stay away from the nonsense, but it was too late. This guy was game and I tore him apart. It was like a starving Sylvester actually catching Tweety Bird and having his way. When the dust cleared, my opponent was cut for 12 and the only blood on me was either his or oozing from my knuckles.

The locals were screaming. I was fuming and now at least mildly satisfied; I had lost the war but had won a personal battle. I must say I didn't expect what happened next. When I looked up, the benches were emptying.

You see, I had grabbed a kid from Slovakia, Vladimir Zak. Tony Iannitto, their GM, had found him a job in Montreal over the summer. He had balls, but he was a typical Euro kid — he was a great player, but as a tough guy he'd rank right up there with Richard Simmons. He'd been game for the tilt, but me grabbing him would be considered gutless by folks in the hockey world. Jesus . . . In all fairness, though, how was I to know? I'd sent my message, but now it was time to pay the piper.

I'd pissed off the wrong people, plain and simple. Two guys in particular were coming at me, shirtless, yelling obscenities, and flexing their turbo-jacked upper bodies with rage. It was as if I had walked into Tony Soprano's living room and pissed on his carpet. I'd bitten off more than I could chew, but I'd made my own bed . . . I had to go down like a man.

Funny thing is, on the floor, people were everywhere. The officials had me tied up and Tony and his coaching staff were holding back their more-than-willing combatants for fear that they'd be suspended for the final. The melee spilled into the dressing room area, but outside of some shoving I managed to get away unscathed. My dad even came down and was ready to join me in combat. Things devolved even further — and even spilled into the parking lot. The yelling continued, but no more punches were thrown. Dad and I and a few pals went back to my place and had a few suds and laughed at the shenanigans.

At that point I moseyed over to the phone to check my messages. What I heard next wiped the cocky smirk off my cleanly shaven mug. The message was simple: "Ryan, we are gonna hunt you down and put a cap in your ass."

I dropped the phone. My motor mouth and rash thinking had gotten me into trouble—again. But this was the kind of trouble that's rarely seen in the cozy confines of a hockey rink. This had to be addressed.

After a few more pops I decided, against my buddies' advice, to go to George Street. I knew they would be out boozing after losing a close game in the final later that day.

It wasn't hard to track down the Montreal guys. I made my way into Etomic, a dance bar on George Street. I made eye contact with one of their guys right away. It was Eric Archambault. I told Eric I wanted to leave what happened on the floor and that I didn't even realize Vladimir was a Slovak. I also apologized for the racist comments. Still, I pointed out, the fight was mutual and so was the trash-talking. I figured I was about to get beat up bad . . . or worse. I gulped in fear of the wolves that began surrounding me.

Well, as is usually the case, cooler heads prevailed and we talked it out. They laughed, told me they just played a prank by leaving the threat on my machine, and asked me to play for them the following year, at the national championships in Montreal. Don't get me wrong, they were pissed by my antics, but they understood why I acted like I did. It was the heat of the moment, and it was in the past now.

Even though they talked hard and played even harder, I grew to become close pals with the Black Knights. I could see where they were coming from and have respect for all of them. So much, in fact, that my wife and a few friends have accompanied the Italians on a trip to their native land a few times. Paolo Musto, our captain, has a place in San Benedetto, Italy, where he, Biaggio Danielle, and Tony hang out every summer.

It's funny how life unfolds. After a crazy day in '02 when I feared for my life, I ended up playing for the Knights for eight years. We finally won the national championship in Vancouver in 2008, and the boys are like my family now. Like the tattoo on my right forearm says, "Knights for Life."

Man, You're Good Lookin'

In mid-February 2007, I was playing senior hockey for the Mount Pearl Blades. It might be my hometown, but that season the hockey was miserable. We had one goalie and two water bottles as the third-place team in a four-team league with fifth-rate fans and half a dozen hangers-on who knew nothing about hockey and just wanted the free beer our sponsors gave us. Far from seventh heaven. Needless to say, it was quite a few steps down from playing for the Habs in the Bell Centre.

My ball hockey career, however, was gaining momentum, and my ankle seemed to hold up better on the floor than the ice. That year I went to Toronto for Team Canada's national selection camp, hoping to win a second World Championship at the upcoming tournament in Düsseldorf, Germany.

The selection camp was exhausting. In many ways, I think you have to be in better shape to play ball hockey. You can't glide like on skates and the stopping and starting is very hard on the joints. After we were done, we were all ready to relax and have a good meal and maybe a few cocktails.

A bunch of us who had been friends since the 2003 World Championship in Switzerland decided to head to a nice Greek restaurant in downtown Toronto and then maybe check out the local scenery at a nearby club. Coach Gortsos is of Greek descent and I remember how happy he was that we decided upon this particular place. George is a great guy with a passion for Canada and everything Canadian. For him, every day is July 1st.

On the way to eat, one of the boys checked out the sports section of the *Toronto Sun* and noticed the Toronto Marlies — the Leafs' AHL affiliate — were playing that particular evening. I called former Red Deer Rebel Brad Leeb, who now played for Marlies, and twisted his rubber arm, and he came out to meet us after his game. We decided on a place and were all in good spirits. I always find it funny when we'd say we'd meet for "one or two" beers. We all knew we were gonna get shit-canned.

When our ball hockey entourage entered the bar, we were already royally fucked up. We knew we wouldn't see each other for a while (we were all flying back to our homes the next day), and we were making the most of the time we had left. Georgie had me on the grappa at dinner, and to be honest, I was shirtless by the time we left. A Canadiens chant of "olé, olé, olé" was accompanied by cheesy high-fives and stories that sounded better while intoxicated. Whistles were directed at any female we saw through the grade-A beer goggles we had going. Many of my buddies in the game of ball hockey are of Italian/Greek/Portuguese descent, and a few have their own restaurants. I love hangin' out with them on nights out that include a meal — it's always a great time.

We ran into the Marlies/Leafs guys as soon as we entered the bar. They weren't as well lit, given that their game had just ended. They were catching up quickly, however. The band was awesome and, considering the state we were in, I felt like the Rolling Stones themselves were playing in my kitchen. I started dancing with myself, doing my best Billy Idol, and then next thing I knew a couple hot babes (beer goggles) were there too. One chick was smokin' and seemed really into me. I found out that a couple of the Marlies had sent her over, and she said she felt like she knew me already. Perfect. "Let's take this to another place," I said, half joking.

I meant my hotel room, but she took me to the washroom. We made out heavier than Vladimir "The Tank" Krutov in 1990 when he ate his way out of the NHL. I opened her shirt, snapped off her bra and frantically pawed her recently purchased, balloon-like breasts. At this point it was time to go to back to my hotel. As I took her out of the bar, I waved as my buddies clapped and laughed.

In her car, my hot young companion and I made out passionately, but it didn't go much further. When she told me it was "that time of the month," it was real hard to take. She was confident and sexy; she had long blond hair, ruby-red lipstick, and wore a tight black tube top, a short tight red skirt, and black fishnets. I irresponsibly dozed off in her car after being shot down.

I remember waking up extremely disoriented. She could have done whatever she wanted, but there we were at my hotel's parking lot—in Brampton. After a long, unconscious drive, I was safe and sound with a stranger, and my money was still in my pocket. She said she was sorry we weren't gonna have sex—but when she said she'd help me get over it with a blow job, I wasn't gonna stop her. I lay back and listened to the radio while she changed my oil. Ten minutes later I was fully serviced and I invited her in. She looked puzzled. I told her she could hang out for a while.

We got out of her car and walked past the security, down the hall, and into my room. A couple of the ball hockey boys had already returned. Their earlier laughter was replaced by bewilderment. What the fuck?

Paolo Musto, our captain and my good friend, grabbed my cheeks like Tony Soprano might. "Terry, are you fucking serious?" he said in his Italian-English accent, shaking his head. "That broad is a dude!"

"Fuck off, Paolo, you're just jealous," I said before near fainting.

Then I looked at "Candy" and realized he might actually be right. I mean, I'd thought she might be a peeler, but never in a million years did I think this broad was carrying ammunition. I began fixating on a horrible thought: in the car, as I kissed her upper lip, I'd found it odd that she seemed to have stubble.

"Why didn't you say anything?" I yelled.

Candy said she had thought I knew.

I had no idea what to do. I wanted to fight, cry, and laugh all at the same time. I also realized that I was first and foremost at an event put on by Team Canada, and any news I could create at two in the morning would be bad news. There was nothing to do but fall back 10 yards and punt, so to speak. After my she-male left and the dust settled, we all stared at each other in silence and I got up and went for a long walk. When I got back, the boys were asleep.

The next morning was awkward, but we laughed after Tony let the elephant out of the room and razzed me to thunderous laughter. If you can believe it, I was a guest on a radio show in Montreal on the TEAM 990 radio that day with Mitch Melnick—as I was every Monday that year—and old the PG version of the tale. (I said I kissed the dude, that was it. They played "Lola" by the Kinks during my segment.) I figured if I just bottled up the story it would still get out and there'd always be rumours, but if I was open and honest it would seem slightly more acceptable. Slightly.

I swear to you, if ever you run into any of the guys that were in attendance that particular February evening, they will tell you that girl looked hot and they were fooled too. But then again, maybe those pricks knew all along . . .

Senior Citizens

Senior hockey has been fun. I've been playing since the 2003–04 season. For those who don't know, the senior level of hockey is the amateur level that comes after junior—it's amateur hockey for adults, 20 and older. Same age as pro. At the top level, it's made up of guys who may have just retired from professional, junior, or college ranks and still want a competitive game, as well as some local players who never left home to pursue bigger hockey goals. I've spent most of my time in the Newfoundland senior hockey circuit, although in 2008 I played for the big bad Bentley Generals of the Alberta league and we went all the way to the Allan Cup final and lost a heartbreaker to Brantford. The game was televised—it was the 100th anniversary of the iconic trophy given to Canada's top amateur men's hockey team, and Walter Gretzky dropped the puck just minutes from the backyard he made famous. Brent Gretzky—Wayne's brother—even played for Brantford that year, so it seemed like they were destined to win. They had a good squad.

When you go to a senior hockey game, you can expect loud fans and passionate hockey. Players make peanuts compared to the pro ranks, so pride is the main motivator. Most guys have to work the next day or attend university classes, so there's a mutual respect for each other as far as cheap shots go (there are many exceptions, of course, and sometimes team pride can cross the fine line into erratic hooliganism). Believe it or not, athletes tend to step it up to higher levels more often in pride's name than for any other reason. Even in pro, if you wanna see guys give it their all, tune in to a Stanley Cup playoff game or an Olympic medal game; the regular season matchups just don't produce the same emotions, and they shouldn't: hockey is a tough sport, and going all-out all the time with the best players in the world 100 times a year isn't possible. Guys tend to give more and take more in the playoffs with winning in mind, not dollar bills.

In senior hockey, every game is like a playoff game because small-town rivalries energize the fan base and the players who want an easy ride are weeded out by the low paycheques. So you are left with a bunch of dogs who love the game so much they'd bleed for it no matter what. A good example of this can be seen in Darren Langdon. Langer was one of the toughest scrappers in hockey for his entire decade-long NHL career. He went about his work respectfully. He fought when he needed to and provided intensity on and off the ice to whatever team needed his attributes and employed him. He treated his teammates like family and did his job honourably.

When Langer plays senior for his hometown Deer Lake Red Wings, he is an animal. The guy will score, slash, fight, goad you into penalties, take the odd questionable penalty himself (to put it mildly), and even find himself suspended. He's my buddy, but during the first senior shift we ever played against each other we ended up getting in a tilt because he hit our goalie, Jeff Murphy. (Afterwards, my face looked like it had been stepped on by a burning cleat.) All that physicality comes from his heart. He loves western Newfoundland — more specifically Deer Lake — and wants the area to succeed. It is a different passion. Most senior teams in Newfoundland use some local talent, who in turn feel a personal association with the team they play for. Although the arenas tend to be small and the team budgets minuscule, everybody plays hard. The monetary rewards are secondary; at the core of the game lies character — and I don't think that should be a huge surprise to anyone.

I am not putting down professionals at all; a guy like Ryan Smyth played hard for his country whenever he was called upon and excels in a playoff atmosphere. He has as much heart as you're ever going to see in any athlete. I am merely pointing out what I see to be the main difference between the two levels of hockey. More people play amateur hockey for love of the game alone. There is something to be said for small-town hockey rivalries in the dead of winter; the sights, smells, and sounds associated with the culture are addictive. Fans love cheering on their local squad, no matter what the league, and then going home to watch their heroes on the tube. NHL players tend to be idols for the kids across the nation, and it was no different when I was a little rink rat. It's a way of life here in Canada and it's one of the reasons I am so proud to have played for the legendary Habs.

Clap for the Wolfman

In 2007, after getting the itch to play professionally again, I thought about trying to give it a shot overseas in one of the European leagues. I've always wanted to see as much of the world as possible, and I thought maybe I could get a game in one of the lesser leagues and take things from there. This seed of an idea never blossomed. I was 30 years old and had to face the fact that my days as an athlete were numbered. My ankle might not have been able to handle a full professional season anyway, and my reflexes, speed, and timing were slowing as I aged. After some soul searching, I quit my job as a Red Bull sales rep, determined to make some kind of change.

At times like this I usually pick up the phone and call on ex-teammates for advice and support. Often this leads to a pal and I having a few drinks together over the phone—solving nothing, but boosting spirits by way of drunken dialogue. Old school players like Jeff Sirkka call this "black-wire fever." Sirk calls me with black-wire fever a few times a year.

One of the first guys I call in these situations is Mark Woolf. Wolfy is seven years older and seems to have gained a wealth of knowledge in those seven years that I sometimes feel I'll never achieve. It's amazing; he's the stereotypical wily-veteran type people feel compelled to be around. He's played in a dozen or more leagues all over Europe and North America and been an impact player wherever he's gone. He loves being part of the community, and because of that Wolfy knows a lot of people in a lot of places and has experience in a wide variety of situations, hockey-related or not. If wisdom is gained from experience, Wolfy is a hockey encyclopedia. He drinks hard liquor and full-bodied beer. He doesn't much care for dance clubs filled with teenyboppers but always relished the times after games when he could have a few pints in a pub with the boys and shoot the shit. Wolfy's everyday speech is laced with proverbs, and his ramblings often double as free lectures. Under a full head of blond hair, scars on his baby face both show his age and reveal his youth all at once. Back when he was with San Diego, Wolfy was often mistaken for a surfer.

"Well, fly out to Calgary. You can stay with me. I hope you like the place, but beggars can't be choosers. I'll help you find a job and we'll play senior hockey somewhere. If a team wants you bad enough, they'll find you something," Wolfy said. "Now get off your ass. We'll figure this out, and I expect to see you soon. As individuals, we all know the right thing to do — the hard part is actually doing it."

This was fine by me. I trusted the Wolfman and knew we'd be holding a better hand as a package than if I just went looking for a place to play on my own. I am a better playmaker than goal scorer, and Wolfy is one of the best snipe-shows I've seen at any level, so we were two-thirds of a good line looking for a place to play. Another huge plus was the fact that I'd have a regimented schedule. Wolfy's dad is a military man, and the apple didn't fall far from the tree. Breakfast was often at the crack of dawn, and every day we worked at odd jobs around his house, like building a fence and a deck in his yard. I had no clue what I was doing, by the way—Wolfy is one of those dudes that always has a wrench in his pocket. He coached me and gave me the easy tasks, like making sure the cooler was full.

It wasn't long before we decided we'd play with the Bentley Generals of the Chinook Hockey League in Alberta. Bentley's organization was full of good people, and they had a shot every year at winning the Alberta men's AAA hockey championship. The famous Sutter brothers had close ties to the team, and Brian even ended up coaching them from 2008–11. Bentley is only about 20 minutes northwest of Red Deer, my old stomping grounds. It had been a decade since I'd played in Red Deer for the Rebels, but I still had many friends there and felt comfortable. It was roughly a 90-minute drive from Wolfy's place in southern Calgary, but we enjoyed the trip and kept each other company. After practices we'd sit in the room and have a beer or two while listening to classic Canadian rock tunes by bands like the Guess Who, the Tragically Hip, and Red Rider. Occasionally, if we'd had one too many to drive home, we'd hit the Monkey Top Saloon and crash at a teammate's place. We had a couch in the dressing room, and I stayed there a few times. Heck, sometimes we'd stay at a fan's place. Bentley is a town of roughly 1,000, and they support the team and each other big time. For a place so small, their success is unprecedented. The Generals have made it to the Allan Cup tournament by winning the McKenzie Cup—a feat accomplished by winning the Alberta hockey championship and then defeating the BC champs—a half dozen times in the past decade. In 2009 the team brought the small town hockey glory by taking home the big prize. They won it again in 2013, on home ice, which must have been awesome for all those diehard fans.

I spent just that one year in Bentley, but it was therapeutic for me to get off the island to play hockey again. I was able to play with some familiar faces from my days back in the WHL—the team drew its roster from Edmonton and Calgary (Red Deer is smack dab in the middle of these two cities) and always had a fantastic nucleus of players. I had former teammates like Dion Darling, Kevin Smyth, and "Sugar" Ray Schultz on the squad, so it immediately felt like home. Ryan Smyth of NHL fame had a close affiliation to the team in that his two brothers, Kevin and Jared, played. Wes Gyori, a well-respected businessman in central Alberta, ran the club. He hooked me and some other guys up with gigs in the oil industry, work that included pipeline and facility construction. We'd do odd jobs, but he paid us well, and it wasn't a problem to ask for time off for games.

Despite losing in the Allan Cup final, I had a blast. In the regular season, I won the Chinook League scoring title, and I had Mark Woolf to thank for that. All I had to do was throw the puck in his direction and I'd end up with an assist! Wolfy and I fed off each other in the regular season, but in the first round of the playoffs versus Fort Saskatchewan I fucked up my shoulder pretty bad. I spent the last couple of months in pain and played okay, but Wolfy picked up my slack like a true leader. Before the second round of the playoffs—a hard-fought seven-game series against Stony Plain—he stood up in the dressing room and reminded us all that even though we had many injuries (our captain, Chad Beagle, was out for the season with a broken leg, I couldn't raise my arm over my head voluntarily, and Joey Vandermeer was playing with a shoulder so painful he'd have to freeze it every period), we had to use the adversity as motivation. "Faith can be dangerous; we have to be certain we are going to win, and work hard to achieve that goal. We can't just believe it's gonna happen. I'm fuckin' old, but that only matters with wine or cheese. We have the team to do this and we have guys on the battleground tonight hurting for us. It's about trust. Do you trust the guy next to you? I sure as fuck do. We need to get to the promised land, boys—and I'm gonna lead us there. Leaders don't know everything, boys; leaders ask questions and learn from experience. Now let's all go out and be fuckin' leaders."

I know, I know—transcribing an amateur hockey dressing room speech may seem ridiculous. But it's important to me to include it because it makes an integral point: all successful teams have their own versions of Mark Woolf, guys who lead by example and are so confident that nothing will intimidate them. This attitude trickles down to the other players, the spares, the staff, and the fans. A good team has no fear because everyone has each other's back. In junior, Wolfy was a sniper, and in 1990–91 he finished third in team scoring on a Spokane Chiefs squad that captured the Memorial Cup championship in Quebec City. The two guys who edged him out on that team? Pat Falloon—a huge talent, who went number two in the 1991 NHL Entry Draft, behind Eric Lindros—and Ray Whitney, who has scored over a thousand points in the Show. Mark's attitude stunk for a while early in his career—Wolfy himself will tell you that. But he learned from his experiences and became a dependable pro with a flair for bringing a dressing room together. He'd energize a room just by showing up. When he spoke, everyone listened.

You already know how this story ends. But the thing is, after the gruelling seven-game series against Stony Plain, we came together even more when we played against Fort St. John, BC, for the McKenzie Cup. We played in their barn in front of a very loud, boisterous crowd and beat them three games to one (in four nights) to capture the Pacific title and earn a berth in the Allan Cup. Wolfy was on fire! He stepped it up to another level in Fort St. John. Injured or not, I played subpar in the Fort, and Wolfy picked me up. The boys then fed off his leadership. The man we called the Wolfman scored two game winners and dished out a few huge hits in the series. I remember how pissed we were when we lost in that final game against Brantford. It had been broadcast on television from coast to coast by TSN. Dejected, nobody spoke for about an hour. The whole season was over and the long road we'd fought through together seemed pointless.

Now, using that experience for my own benefit, I know that season was far from pointless. We fought hard together, won two championships, and earned a silver medal in a national championship after a very difficult playoff. We faced adversity all year and played through multiple injuries and multiple elimination games. We made it as far as we did because we played for each other—we were certain we weren't gonna lose, because we were certain the guy next to us was gonna get the job done.

The next season, I returned home to play for the Corner Brook Royals of the Newfoundland League after working out a deal with all-around good guy Wally Fitzpatrick, ex-firefighter and their GM at the time. I would live in Red Deer and they'd fly me to Corner Brook every weekend to play for the Royals! I'd stay with local superfans Sean and Nancy Gibbons (now godparents to my daughter, Penny-Laine) at the bottom of picturesque Marble Mountain, nestled in the heart of Steady Brook, not far from where my rock 'n' roll buddy Brian Byrne grew up. They also paid me a decent salary, and my parents got to see me play again, so it was nice. The move was unprecedented, though, and I still can't believe I did all that flying every week. On Thursday evenings, I'd drive over an hour to Calgary, fly to Toronto, fly to Halifax, and then to Deer Lake, Newfoundland. At least 12 hours one way, usually more, and often double that. If I was lucky I'd catch a red-eye and not have to stop in Halifax. I'd drive to Corner Brook, another half hour or so, and go to the rink and suit up that night. On Monday I'd do the whole thing in reverse, often hungover. The time in the air actually paid off—I ended up piecing a lot of this book together on those trips!

I had a great time out west, but felt my itch was scratched; I was ready to settle back into living close to my family on the Rock, so Danielle, Ty, and I made the move east. Eventually I had a part to play in helping Newfoundland get back to playing in the Allan Cup, and in 2011 the Clarenville Caribous became the first team from the province of Newfoundland to win the famed trophy since the Corner Brook Royals in 1986.

Wolfy came to Newfoundland for the last part of the 2008–09 season and finished his career playing on my line in Corner Brook. We had a close mutual pal named Darren Colbourne who played with us as well, and he and Wolfy were very close in pro and are the same age. They hadn't seen each other in a long time, and even though we lost in the first round of the playoffs, it was magic to play with a legend I respected so much, in his final season playing the game he loved.

The Bentley Generals won the Allan Cup that year in Steinbach, Manitoba—one season after we lost in the final game. Wolfy and I watched the game at a bar on 17th Avenue in Calgary. We shed some tears of joy as the boys paraded the trophy around the ice—we still felt like part of that team. The guys had built off of the experiences of the year before and come back stronger and more prepared.

During their celebration, I glanced at Wolfy and saw him smiling ever so slightly as he sipped on his rum and coke. He wasn't jealous; he was satisfied, contented. Mark knew that his speech and leadership from the year before contributed to the Generals' monumental victory. He knew the boys knew it too, and that's all he cared about. We hugged, acknowledging what had just happened, and put down our empty glasses. Nothing more needed to be said. Then we went fishing.

The Conception Bay Comeback

This book has been "complete" four or five times. Each time I submit a final draft, it seems, someone reminds me of a story that took place in the past, and I feel obligated to include it. Some stories feel like they just have to be told, and any memoir I write would be incomplete without them. The following is one of those tales, except as I was finishing the book I was actually living this story. It played out right in front of me and was such a fantastic experience I had to not only mention it but devote an entire chapter to it.

You see, the 2012–13 hockey season was likely to be my last as a player, and things were generally negative all round as the year progressed through the first stages of the schedule. My team, the Conception Bay CeeBees, were playing way below expectations. We were in last place at the Christmas break. I had just graduated from university but couldn't find a job anywhere. Danielle was experiencing hiccups trying to get her maternity clothing line, PennyPosh, off the ground and was irritable much of the time (it has since successfully launched!). Our family struggled to make ends meet, and I was busted up a lot—injuries that I played through but not without pain. For months, I bled when I took a piss because I hadn't let a kidney shot heal the right way. Other guys were getting injured more than normal. The weather seemed miserable all the time. Danielle and I argued a lot due to the compounded stress these issues produced. The team bus broke down every trip, highlighted by a 27-hour journey home from Grand Falls (usually four hours) in a winter storm. We lost 9, 10, 11 games in a row . . . things were dismal. Everything I touched on the ice was poison.

Then, one day in early January, it all changed. Everything. A complete 180 so incredible you really had to be there and see it to appreciate it. It changed my life, in a way, but I am getting ahead of myself here. Let me explain.

In roughly a decade playing senior hockey, I had only ever played for the Mount Pearl Blades and Corner Brook Royals in the Newfoundland League, save for that one great year with Wolfy and company in 2007–08 in Bentley, Alberta. Mount Pearl is my hometown and I am very proud of that — it's a great little family community — but as far as supporting senior hockey, it has never been successful. In the four years I played there, we had a full barn (approximately 2,000 people) maybe twice — both times in rare playoff appearances. Nothing against Harry Bartlett and Jim Hare, our owner and general manager. They were good guys and tried, but we just didn't get the support we needed to run a senior hockey team. We were usually last in league attendance, averaging only a few hundred per game, and when there are teams in the league like Grand Falls, with over 900 season ticket holders, they tend to be attractive destinations for players for that reason alone. More fans also equals more profit, so players are treated better on successful teams. This is simple business of course, and that is why Mount Pearl lost their squad for the 2012–13 season, and all of its players — including me—were put into a dispersal draft amongst the five remaining teams: the Western Royals, the Clarenville Caribous, the Grand Falls–Windsor Cataracts, the Gander Flyers (an expansion team), and the Conception Bay North (CBN) CeeBees.

To make a long story short, the CeeBees acquired myself and my good pals Grant Kenny and Jason Hedges from the Blades, along with our exuberant equipment manager, David "Ropedog" Roper. Ropedog is as much a part of the team as anyone else and is great in the room. Sometimes the trainers and equipment guys are the glue that brings a team together, and smart coaches know that and pick the right people for the gig. Hedgy, GK, Ropedog, and I had been teammates in the past for multiple years, but only Grant had ever won the coveted Herder Memorial trophy—the NLSHL's version of the Stanley Cup—as a member of the Clarenville Caribous in the late 2000s. I had won a provincial senior hockey title, yes, but it was in Alberta with Bentley. I didn't have a Herder.

In Newfoundland, the Herder is hockey's Holy Grail and goes back to the mid-1930s. Many hockey fans around here know more about the history of the Herder and local hockey legends than they do about the NHL, and that is no exaggeration. I love this, by the way. I think a lot of it comes from the isolation of living on an island. Everyone knows everyone, and most people have a relative or friend involved with local amateur sports on some level. The Herder finals, if played at Mile One Centre in beautiful downtown St. John's, which holds upwards of 7,000 people per game, is routinely sold out. Face-painters and team signs are commonplace. The booze is usually sold out by the end of the second period too, which may give you some idea of the energetic, boisterous atmosphere senior playoff hockey can generate.

I should also point out that the CeeBees are as historic as the Herder itself. The team goes back well over half a century, and in the early days was led by brothers George and Alex Faulkner, two of the best players of their era. Alex was actually scouted right from a local exhibition game against some NHLers. He got invited to Toronto Maple Leafs camp and ended up playing professionally for over a decade, highlighted by a 100-game stint with the Detroit Red Wings between 1962 and 1964. The CeeBees had won the Herder trophy eight times; first in 1960 and most recently in 2008. The community itself is also steeped in tradition, being one of the oldest settled areas in all of North America. Cupids (part of CBN) and Jamestown, Virginia, are the oldest settled British colonies in the continent, dating back to the early 1600s. In a nutshell, CBN is a town soaked in traditional values, and the locals support their own like a family and expect results. I had always wanted to play there, and I consider it an honour to be a part of their history.

In early January, we were in last place. Every game, we found a way to lose. We dropped a dozen in a row, and with only a few games left in the regular season we found ourselves in a tie for the fourth and final playoff position with the expansion Gander Flyers; it was coming down to the wire. Our executive had brought in a lot of talent at the dawn of the season in order to bring winning ways back around the Bay, but we were failing miserably. We had a great hockey team on paper, made up of many players, young and old, with some impressive resumes: Robert Slaney (24, played for Hamilton in the AHL in '11–12), Keith Delaney (33, Florida Panthers draft pick), Doug O'Brien (former QMJHL top defenceman and NHLer with Tampa), Jordan Escott (21, QMJHL), Ray Dalton (33, QMJHL), Chris Sparkes (28, ECAC) . . . just to name a few. Mike Dyke and Donnie Gosse were both big, bruising, talented defencemen who had been all-stars in the Newfoundland League for the better part of a decade. Our goalie was Mark Yetman, 24, who had been a starter with Halifax of the QMJHL. Our imports were 33-year-old defenceman Nick "The Train" Theriault—a big (6-foot-4,

235 pounds), bruising former pro who gave no free passes out there, using his stick like an axe at times — and Chris "the Cannon" Hulit. Chris sniped a lot of goals in his OHL and Canadian Interuniversity career, and at 28 was still in shape and in his prime. With this roster, we were underachieving big-time. Attendance was dwindling and rumours of folding surfaced here and there. I was embarrassed. We were all embarrassed. This was supposed to be the year that glory was brought back to CBN.

One Wednesday night we were greeted by the members of the executive after practice. There were three weekends left in the regular season, and the team was in major financial trouble. They told us we were supposed to leave for Deer Lake — a five- or six-hour drive — on Saturday morning, but apparently we didn't have enough money to do so. A typical road weekend costs between 10 and 15 thousand dollars, and our well had run dry a long time ago. If not for some members of the executive bailing us out in recent times, we'd have folded at Christmas. When they first brought in all the outside talent, they thought things would go well. They thought we'd have more success on the ice and at the gate. Essentially, I was part of a group of people who were brought in to help the team but were effectively hurting it. The executive gave us a decision — play for free or fold.

I know what you some of you are thinking. It's senior hockey — these guys should be happy to get paid at all! Well, yes and no. Yes, we are happy we got paid to play, but the league is now run like a pro league, and that has to be respected. Players are expected to be in top shape and devote a huge portion of time to their team. There are only 24 games guaranteed, so do the math. Many players, including myself, have families, and we rely on the money to get by. In my case, the senior hockey paycheque put me through university.

I have to give our leaders credit. It would have been easy to quit. Players like Ryan Delaney, Gosse, Dyke, and Freddy Diamond had been around awhile and were busy with school/work/family, but they wanted to play. Younger fellas like Colin Escott, Colin Feehan, Freddy Earle, and Danny "Judas" Sparkes were all in. Jamie Tobin and Steve "Goat" Greeley looked at me and grinned. I wanted to play too—we'd put so much into this thing, and we had great people surrounding us. Keith Delaney was our captain—and a great captain at that—and he led us in a long conversation with the executive, laying out some rules and guidelines for the rest of the season. No matter which way we sliced it, we were going to have to play most of the remainder of the season pro bono.

The executive let go of our coach, Cory Crocker, too, which was unfortunate, but sometimes shit happens, I guess. Cory is from the CBN area, and he did some great work recruiting players—including myself—but we were flying him in from Amherst, Nova Scotia, every weekend, and with a 4–17 record I suppose a change of atmosphere that also cuts costs becomes a priority. He's still our buddy, and just by recruiting alone, Cory helped shape our team. He believed in us from day one and we know that.

The next four games were somewhat optimistic; we dropped two of them outright, but we gained a point for a shootout loss in Deer Lake and won a game in a shootout in Grand Falls. We outshot our opponent in each of those games and seemed to be turning a corner. We were playing for each other now, down but not out, and the results were slight at first but noticeable. Gander had to beat us twice on the last weekend, on our home ice in S.W. Moores Stadium, but we came back from a 3–1 deficit halfway through the first game to win 5–3 and solidify our place in the playoffs. After a disastrous regular season, our record was 7–15–1 heading into the playoffs, and we were set to face off against the Grand Falls–Windsor Cataracts, a team that had just cued up one of the best regular seasons in the history of the league, with 20 wins, 3 losses, and 1 shootout loss.

The first two games of the best-of-seven series were played in Grand Falls on a Friday and Saturday in mid-February. Both were hard-fought battles, and after the first weekend of play the series was tied 1–1. Even though we had dropped the second game 6–2 after winning the first in overtime off the stick of ex-QMJHL 36-goal scorer Robert Slaney, we were happy with the split. We were going back to our own barn. The fans would be ready to cheer us on after we saved face by making the playoffs and giving them a little more hockey to watch, if nothing else. It isn't easy for a visiting team to win on a tiny ice surface in front of a packed house at SW Moores Stadium, and with a relatively full lineup for the first time all season, we were looking as good or better than we had all year. We were big and mean — especially our defence, at an average height of over 6-foot-3 — and played better in a small arena, where our foot speed wasn't exposed like it would have been on a big ice surface. If we could contain the Cataracts forwards, we'd have a decent shot at winning both games; if not, another split wouldn't be entirely bad, considering most people had us written off in four straight before the playoffs started. If we lost both, it would be all over heading back to the Falls.

Game three was a close battle, with each team getting some great scoring chances. The power plays were relatively even, the shots were close, and the goalies — former Canadian Interuniversity backstop and league MVP A.J. Whiffen for Grand Falls, and Mark Yetman for us — stood on their heads. Fans were squashed together like sardines, and around 30 seconds into overtime, "Sugar" Ray Dalton sent Mike McCarthy, Tracey Shute, and the rest of CeeBee Nation into a frenzy with a Mario Lemieux–like wrist shot over A.J.'s shoulder, up under the crossbar, and into the top corner of the net. The barn erupted, and I was first on the scene. I squeezed Sugar Ray like he was a ripe orange and I was a juicer. We were up 2–1 in round one of the historic Herder playoffs, and feeling the positive energy vibrate through the building after such a tumultuous few months would give anyone goosebumps, I don't care who you are. We were far from winning the series, though, and had to contain our emotions. After all, game four was less than 24 hours away.

TR on the IR

The next day, we all got to the rink early, played some music, and focused on the task at hand. Not much needed to be said. This game was massive. If we won, we'd be up 3–1 and have a stranglehold on the series. If we lost, it would be 2–2 going back to Grand Falls, where they won all but two games all season. When we came out for warm-up, we were greeted with a standing ovation. Hecklers heckled and rattled their rattlers. As the Zamboni made its way around the ice for the last turn before the game got underway, I peered out the dressing room door at the latecomers jockeying for seats and settling for standing room. Two particularly courageous boys hung from one of the rafters by the radio booth. CeeBees jerseys peppered the crowd, and most fans wore our team colours of blue, red, and white. Cody Penney and Maxwell Butler—two of our biggest fans—sent me a message before the game, and it was made up of only one word: BELIEVE. Hockey fever was back in Harbour Grace.

By the middle of the second period, we were up by a goal. Our line—myself, Chris Sparkes, and Sugar Ray—was playing well, and

Sparky already had more goals in this series than he'd scored all season. I remember hearing the loudspeaker blare, "Tonight's 50/50 is now over $2,500" before a faceoff, and chuckling. Sugar Ray lost the draw and I tried getting a head start on covering my man, pit-bullish ex-pro Colin Power, but slipped. My knee was bruised from the game before, and I couldn't put as much weight on it as I'd like. No biggie, I had a painkiller in me and didn't feel much. I got up and started skating towards my own end, where the play was quickly developing. All of a sudden I heard a snap, felt a thud on my back, and fell to the ice. One of the bigger Cataracts defencemen — Greg Hoffe, who weighed 240 pounds or so — had given me a shot in the ribs behind the play, and I didn't feel right. I skated to the bench and hid the pain as best I could, although Gussy French, one of our trainers, noticed me flinching. He recommended I stay on the bench and skip my next shift to catch my breath, but I ignored him, thinking it was just a bump and I'd get through it. I knew something was up, though.

Shortly after I got out for my next shift, I tried to dump the puck into the offensive zone with a slapshot, and it was lights out. I collapsed and couldn't breathe. I heard GFW forward Andrew Pearcey telling me I'd better get off the ice, I didn't look so well. Within seconds I was gasping for air, to no avail. I tasted metal as I gasped. I looked down and spit. It wasn't metal I tasted, it was blood. There was red spatter all over the ice, and I was in trouble. I gathered myself, skated off, and tried to chat with Dr. Jared Butler, who was standing next to our dressing room. I still couldn't breathe right, though, and I jumped in the car of family friend Patty O'Keefe with my hockey gear on, and we drove to Carbonear General Hospital.

Within minutes I was on a hospital bed with a tube inserted in my side, designed to help me breathe correctly and remove the blood from my lungs. Apparently Hoffer — who is a friend and has since apologized — had punctured my lung after breaking a couple of ribs with the hit to my upper back on my right side. When I tried to keep playing, I drove my rib in further and collapsed my lung completely. Shit. I was disappointed, but all I could think about was the game. Did we win? How could I find out if we won?

I grabbed my cell phone. The only place I could get a signal was in one of the public bathrooms on the second floor. It wasn't easy getting used to carrying around a sack full of blood attached to my body by a tube, but I eventually wedged myself in between a toilet and a sink. As I jostled my phone around, I finally found a signal. I called my father, who was at home babysitting Penny-Laine, and after I explained to him that I was okay, he held the phone up to the broadcast. The game was tied, again in overtime. As I closed my eyes and listened to the brilliant play-by-play of Mr. George Scott, I was sent airborne with excitement when I heard, "Dalton has done it again! Dalton scores in overtime for the second night in a row!" I jumped up so hard I slammed my already banged-up knee on the sink and reinjured the fuckin' thing, but I didn't give a shit. I was coming to the realization that I was likely out for the year anyway. We were up 3–1, and that's what mattered most. The ball was in our court. We were a win away from upsetting the Cataracts — a convincing regular season champion — and vindicating ourselves and our fans for such a tremendously terrible regular season.

To make a long story short, the Cats kicked our asses in game five back at the Joe Byrne Stadium. I think it was like 8–2, but I don't remember much about it because, due to my fresh injury, I was lying down in the dressing room for most of the game, listening to the play-by-play. We were never really in it, we played tentative and nervous, and their fans were extremely loud after every hit, shot, or goal. They took the momentum early and kept it all game. We did send a small message — there were a few scuffles at the end of the game and a couple of good tilts. We knew we'd played shitty, and now we needed to get the fuck outta there and focus on winning at home. Game six was the following evening, and we had a long bus ride, so we played a few games of cards on the bus and ate good food, starting to prepare for battle the next day. Nobody said anything, but it was gonna be hard to beat the Cataracts back in the confines of the Joe Byrne if we came back for game seven. Even though we were ahead in the series, the next evening was a must-win.

Without exhausting you with details about the next day, I'll tell you we were greeted to a thunderous ovation by the crowd back home the next evening, and there was a nice buzz throughout the community. Fans spilled over the boards in warm-up. I wasn't in the lineup — I'd been told I would be on the shelf for 8 to 10 weeks, and the pain fit accordingly. It killed me not to be battling with my pals out there, but that frustration was wiped out by excitement at the possibility that we might win this series and go on to play for the Herder.

The game was tight for most of the way, but we definitely used our home ice to our advantage. Our coach, Ian Moores, told us to go out and hit everything that moved; the fans would make noise, but we had to create every chance for them to do so or we'd waste this home-ice opportunity. We took the advice, and the crowd was noisy all game. After the first period we were up 2–1. After the second period it was 3–1 CeeBees. As time ticked away, the reality of the situation hit home. With eight minutes remaining on the clock, we were up 4–2. Comfortable, but not a guarantee.

Then all of a sudden a Cataracts slapshot hit a stick in front of our net and deflected up into the air, hitting 6-foot-5 forward Chris Sparkes directly in the face, tearing it open and creating two flaps instead of one lip. When Sparky came off the ice, me and a few of the guys who were scratched tried helping him in the dressing room, but he was a bloody mess. Dave Regular, another one of our trainers, told him to get undressed and we'd take him to hospital, but Sparky was having none of that. He said stitches would take too long. There was no doctor on hand to stitch him up, and it seemed like there was nothing we could do — the referees told us the bleeding had to be stopped before he would be allowed back on the ice.

"Fuck that," Sparky shouted. "If I go back out there the place will go bonkers and we'll ride the momentum! The boys will love it!"

I told Sparky to settle down and accept the fact he couldn't get back out there, and then all of a sudden the crazy fucker pointed to a stapler sitting on the dressing room table and told Dave to help him staple his face together and get him a "glob of Vaseline to slow down the bleeding." One of the boys stuck a couple of staples in Sparky's face and Ropedog rushed to get a full cage screwed onto his helmet in the place of his half-visor. Sparky was bleeding like a stuck pig but we managed to slow it down by adding a baseball-sized glob of Vaseline to his yapper. He looked at me, smiled, and stood up. His face was mangled. I mean, Sparky is a good-lookin' dude, but right then he looked like a monster from a horror movie. He proceeded towards the door, waited for a whistle, hopped back on the ice, and that was that. In all my years I've never ever seen anything like it. Picture how much adrenaline must be running through someone's veins, and how much courage it requires for a person — who also is a prominent businessman in his everyday life — to take a stapler to one of the most sensitive areas of his body. All for the boys. Jesus, I still can't believe what I saw. Chris Sparkes, the MacGyver of hockey lacerations, with balls the size of grapefruits.

When Sparky returned to the ice with around five minutes left, loud got louder. People looked at him skating back towards the bench and started standing up, cheering in appreciation. They applauded for the remainder of the game. Sparky's display of heart and soul via the battered face summed it all up. As people looked on in disbelief, I realized that what just happened was a metaphor for our whole season. Resilience, determination, overcoming adversity, grit . . . all of it. Sparky thought stitches would take too long, and he wanted to get out there and play; a reminder that just like our season, there is no easy way out, and the road to the promised land isn't always a pretty one. The Grand Falls bench looked on, stunned. The game was over, and they knew it. The nail had been hammered into the coffin. I can relate to their frustration; they played hard, but no matter what, it just seemed like our destiny to win. As we skated off the ice, it was like we'd won the Stanley Cup, after just a single playoff round! The night we won that series was one of the better memories I've had in my life.

The next series we faced the 2011 Allan Cup–winning Clarenville Caribous, and, in a nutshell, we dominated. On March 16, 2013, I finally had my Herder championship. We completed the biggest comeback in the history of the coveted trophy by winning the league final in four games, sweeping the defending champs while riding the emotion generated by the first series. I even got into a game; I dressed for game three and Boiler (Ian Moores) threw me in for a half-dozen shifts to get the crowd on their feet (painkillers get a bad rap, but they worked miracles for me this game), and luckily enough I came out of it in one piece. Clarenville did have their moments — they played hard, and two of the games could have gone either way — but we weren't going to be denied the ultimate prize. We hit more, blocked more shots, stitched up more flesh, and iced more bruises. As GK pointed out before game four, there were three guys in the room with injuries so bad they couldn't tie their skates (Colin Feehan had a shoulder separation, Jamie

Tobin had a broken hand, and my ribs wouldn't allow for me to cough hard, much less tie skates), yet we all wanted to play that night. Tobes got to play because he hadn't been in the series yet, and I couldn't argue with that. My ribs were paining bad, and I was still pissing blood. The adversity we faced taught us how to win, and once we believed in ourselves, anything was possible.

When I was handed the trophy after the game, I raised it with immense pride. I had played so long and hard for the opportunity to hoist the Herder. I grew up watching local hockey heroes and hearing the folklore of the whole thing; it was legendary in my eyes and had been ever since I was a four-year-old and watched my dad play for the Stephenville Jets. I know it may seem a little over the top that I put so much time and energy into something like a provincial hockey trophy, but Newfoundlanders know where I am coming from. On top of all this, the way we won the Herder was truly an outstanding achievement of the human spirit. I've won a lot of championships in a few different sports at this point, and this was a unique experience. One of my proudest moments — and ironically, I barely played in the final. Jesus Christ, how can you not love hockey.

Why did I choose to go into so much detail about the 2013 Conception Bay CeeBees Herder run? Well, I think many of the messages and themes I touch on in this book are well represented in that story. A month before the season ended, our organization nearly folded, but we all got together and decided to give it a shot and play for free; we wanted to give ourselves a chance, at least, and even though things were playing out rather negatively at the time, we always, always believed in ourselves. We had great leaders, and they stepped up big time. Experience is a factor people tend to underestimate, and it's one thing we oozed — we had the oldest team in the league by far. We loved each other. How many league awards did we get? Zero. How many players finished in the top 10 in league scoring? Nada. All my individual accomplishments pale in comparison. I'd much rather my children shape their character out of stories like this than any of my own personal achievements. What a fantastic game. Amen.

Why I Love the Game

Hockey's an easy game to fall in love with. Its players are, for the most part, good-natured people who appreciate things. It's filled with small-town guys who make it big—or not. Guys who are easy to deal with as far as the media and fans go, who seem to appreciate the fact that that they get to do what they love and earn a living, if only for a short time. Hockey's also a sport where a character slip-up—whether it be a goal celebration, an unfair hit, or any level of disrespect—can result in bare-knuckle fighting. Even for the finesse guys, just to continue playing knowing that this is a reality, and that at any minute you may be hit by a guy who's 6-foot-5 and 230 pounds—well, you have to have some character and level of toughness.

In my mind, hockey may be the most difficult pro sport to play. It definitely is if you are only comparing it to the other three North American team sports. And here's why I think this way.

Physicality

The sport is always physical. You are constantly getting hit—hard. Shift after shift, for 60 minutes. Stoppages of play are infrequent and don't last long, and the average player's size is more than 6-foot and 200 lbs. On top of that, you are skating, not running, while hitting and being hit. Changes happen on the fly, so players are constantly in motion. The faster you skate, the harder the hit. Basketball has an underrated level of physicality—but it doesn't allow bodychecking. Baseball, well, baseball is baseball. Football is very physical, obviously. But it's based on short plays and there are extra long stoppages. Players are bigger, yes, but if an NHLer tried some of those hot-dog celebrations football players are famous for? He'd have to answer the bell. I am not saying football players aren't tough. They are huge, and some are very mobile. But it's all relative. When you go into another team's barn and hear all the screaming fans and know you may have to bare-knuckle fight, trust me, it's intimidating. I celebrated goals here and there, but if I had ever taken out a Sharpie and signed the puck à la Terrell Owens, for example, I'd have been digging my own grave. Someone would have put the beat-down on me right away.

The Schedule

Professional hockey players play around 100 games a year—82 regular season games plus exhibition and playoffs. Let's just look at the regular season schedules and compare.

Baseball: 162. A lot of games to play, no doubt. Let's face it, it's definitely tough to make the major leagues, as there are more players worldwide, but as far as physicality goes, baseball comes last. Although I would take guys like Pete Rose and Derek Jeter on my team any day. I love watching Brett Lawrie with the Jays, who plays with a childlike passion and makes every game entertaining by going his hardest.

Football: 16. This is where hockey takes over. Any argument for football it ends here. 16 games. We have 82. 'Nuff said.

Basketball: 82. I've always said that people underrate this sport on the toughness scale. These guys are huge, and there are more cheap shots going down under that hoop than on ladies' night in a rundown strip club. This is a tough schedule too. But with 60-minute games and only one time out, hockey trumps hoops.

Hockey Players Carry a Weapon

Never mind bodychecking, try getting whacked in front of the net with a piece of lumber (or graphite, aluminum, whatever) and staying there, knowing you are gonna get hit more. Plus, while we might be wearing equipment, there is not much padding on the back of your body, and that's exactly where guys like Chris Pronger or Shea Weber make you pay. Night in, night out, even the skill guys get whacked and pay the price.

There Is No Out of Bounds

The boundaries in hockey are marked by boards and hard glass, not paint. So not only are you getting hit, most of the time you are getting sandwiched between an opposing player and a wall with almost no give. In other sports, running out of room means you leap out of bounds and wait for the play to start again. In hockey, running out of room routinely results in getting hit hard from a large human being who is *skating*, not running, making the hit that much more devastating. Like my pal Sean Wadden always says, "You can run out of bounds in the NFL, but in the NHL the boards act as another defender—there's nowhere to fuckin' go, boys! Our game is tougher, period." Very true, Wads.

The Playoffs

For those who haven't done it, watch the Stanley Cup playoffs. For those who have, watch closer. Four rounds of best-of-seven means it takes a lot of guts to win a championship. Also, combine all of what I've written above and multiply it. More games in less time, more hits, more slashes, more bruises. Fewer fights, though—and I understand that. Even though I did a lot of fighting as a player, I think it slows the game down in playoffs. But there still is a place for it. I recommend watching Jarome Iginla and Vincent Lecavalier go at it in the 2004 Stanley Cup final. Two franchise players fighting for hockey's ultimate prize and doing whatever it takes. High emotion levels from two guys who played together on Team Canada. Bottom line: hockey has the most gruelling playoff grind, by a wide margin.

Intangibles

The speed, skill, and finesse of hockey are highly underrated. Remember, you can be the best stickhandler in the world or able to run a four-minute mile, but in order to even consider playing at a high level, you have to be able to skate! Skating is hard enough to master on its own, but throw in passing, shooting, hitting, defence, and on-ice awareness, and it really is a game that requires an ultra-high level of smarts and athleticism. Watching Alexander Ovechkin or Sidney Crosby drive to the net is like watching an artist at work—actually, it *is* watching an artist at work! Some of those old Gretzky and Lemieux highlights still make my jaw drop. I played against each of those legends once, and both memories are sublime.

I'm sure you can tell how passionate I am about hockey, but the same ideas lie at the heart of any team game. I believe parents should consider putting their kids in a team atmosphere; it teaches them good values. Hockey is just one option. In fact, one of my better sports memories is playing with my Mount Pearl Storm in the St. John's city baseball playoffs a couple of years ago. We played the Knights in a best-of-five semifinal series and were in the fifth and deciding game. The Knights tied the game in the last inning, and we ended up playing a marathon 18 innings—over six hours—setting a league record in the process. I ended up going a whopping 0-for-9, striking out four times and popping up twice with a guy on third and none out. We won, though, with Adam "La-La" Lawlor scoring from third on a balk in the bottom of the 18th, and my dismal day at the plate ended in high-fives all around. Nothing beats winning as a team, no matter what sport, no matter what level.

I should also point out that I use the word "guys" because it is relevant to my experience, but I am also very proud of our Canadian female hockey players, who continue to be the best in the world. Women like Cassie Campbell and Hayley Wickenheiser have led a generation of Canadian female hockey players into the 21st century with a winning attitude and positive mindset; they've shown young women across the country (and the world) that being a world champion or television sportscaster isn't just possible, it is becoming commonplace.

As a coach/scout, I've helped develop the female ball hockey game within the country and province, and the sport is catching on fast all over the planet. In fact, in June 2013 I watched the Canadian female ball hockey team win a gold medal at the world championship here in St. John's, and I can assure you it was one of the best games of any kind I've ever seen. Dawn Tulk from Deer Lake, Newfoundland, scored both goals in a 2–0 victory over Slovakia, continuing Canada's tradition of world dominance in all things hockey. Most fans in the crowd not only cheered and waved our flag proudly, they were weeping tears of joy as they did so.

The Last Word

There you have it — the life tales of someone you likely have never heard of. I could go on talking about my hockey journey forever, because I thoroughly enjoy yakking about the game, and I truly feel honoured to have played, even briefly, for the world-famous Montreal Canadiens. At the core of the game I love are sacrifice, trust, and loyalty — things that I believe are essential to simply living life itself.

Still, I know what some people are gonna think. Some are going to say "Another washed-up attention-grabber pullin' a Canseco and writing a tell-all to make a few bucks . . ."

Well, for one thing, this is far from a tell-all. I'll point out the obvious, now: this isn't anything like Jose Canseco selling out his pals when he released *Juiced*. I am the only one who looks like a jackass in these stories.

Secondly, I wanted to be as honest as I could so people could see the hockey world through the eyes of someone who has nothing to lose — if I had been an NHL star I probably couldn't get away with some of what lies between these covers.

Finally, there isn't a huge amount of coin in being the author of exactly one Canadian book. If I were a big football or basketball star in the States, I could release 200 pages of hogwash and have it top the bestseller list, but dressed-up stories about an ex-prospect who plays amateur sports and lives in Newfoundland don't tend to grab the attention of Howard Stern or Kelly Ripa. Well, maybe Stern . . . But I'd have to blow a goat or something once I got to his studio.

I'm clearly not going to get rich or become famous after releasing this nugget of Canadian literature, so that's not my motivation. To be quite honest with you, I'm doing this because of the advice my parents gave me when I was a teenager leaving home to pursue my dream. They told me to keep a journal, to write down my experiences — it was a big regret my father had about his playing days. He saved souvenirs of all kinds but never wrote anything down, and he figures he lost a lot of memories because of this. I listened to him, and I'm glad I did. As time rolled by and my hockey career took me on an emotional and physical roller coaster, I always had my journal with me. Because of this I always had stories to read to the boys on long bus or plane rides — and after years of compiling I had more than enough tales to fill a book.

Why *Tales of a First-Round Nothing*? Well, it's a bit of a

pun—chatting with Ron MacLean has rubbed off on me over the years, I guess. (He's the punniest guy I know.) When I was in grade school, I used to read stories by Judy Blume. She had a series of children's books that focused on a boy named Peter Hatcher and his little brother Farley, a.k.a. "Fudge." The first book of the series is called *Tales of a Fourth Grade Nothing*. Peter often caused mischief, but he had a good heart and was usually misunderstood. I related to him—and not only because I was a bit of a shit-disturber. I always felt like I was on the outside of something—maybe that has something to do with being an only child—and moving to British Columbia at such a young age magnified this feeling. I can't really say it's a bad thing, because I feel unique and I love being different. In my opinion, one of the saddest things in life is to see someone once vibrant get into a dull routine and accept it. Maybe that's why I have so many stories; I always felt like I had something to prove, and I enjoy the thought of adventure. I wanted to take advantage of every single situation. Whatever the case, I am also a social butterfly, so the road I've chosen has paid off. I have met a lot of people and shared a lot of great experiences because I can play a game well.

My son Tison will be 15 and my daughter Penny-Laine will be 4 when this is finally released. Some people probably wonder what kind of message a book filled with so many R-rated stories is sending my kids. Some will say I am a bad parent. Fuck 'em. I'll answer those critics right now.

Tison is his own person, and I treat him with respect. I love him and I know his biological father, BJ, would be proud of him—more because of what a great young man he has become than the amount of goals he gets this season. Tison is a smart kid—as is Penny-Laine—and I'd much rather they pursue school than any sport. Ty is proud of me and has heard these stories before. Penny-Laine will hear them eventually. Tison and Penny-Laine have seen me dedicate countless hours to getting a university degree, and I am happy to finally say I'll have my bachelor of arts, with a folklore major and English minor, by the time this book is released. My kids know that being loose-lipped about my experiences can be my Achilles heel, but that underneath the thin mask of anecdotes and punchlines there are important themes in this book that will only become more crucial the older they get. If you treat your team like your family, you'll get further in any game you choose to immerse yourself in, and that spills over into the everyday world: sports are a metaphor for life.

Normally there's a special section for thank-yous, but I want to make an exception here as my book winds down and thank my family and every other family out there who supports amateur sports. Making money playing professionally is one thing, but having the opportunity to compete at a high level isn't possible for many adults due to commitments like work, family, and hobbies. If you see an aging veteran in the twilight of his career, like me, wheeling around the ice in a senior hockey game, chances are he has a tight support system. Since I've turned 30, I've made great memories and won top amateur-level championships in baseball, ball hockey, and ice hockey, and I am very aware of the sacrifices my family makes that allow these things to happen. It really hit home couple of years ago when Danielle's parents, Bruce and Lorraine, flew across the country to babysit so I could attend the National Ball Hockey Championships. And if it weren't for Danielle and my parents, this book would never have seen the light of day. They did what they could to ensure I pursued my goal, finished my degree, and released *Tales of a First-Round Nothing*.

I'll finish with something I mentioned at the beginning of the book—it seems fitting.

I love the game: the team concept, the finesse, the toughness, the camaraderie . . . the whole experience. The game is beautiful. Most of life's important lessons can be taught not only on the ice but in the values that make a player a good teammate off of it. Learning to win is about learning to lead and succeed through unity. It requires acts of unselfishness that make you not only a better player but a better person. Hockey imitates life because the attributes it takes to be successful on the ice mirror the realities of the everyday grind. Life is full of ups and downs—and so is a hockey career. Learning to deal with it can be difficult and rewarding.

I feel rewarded.

That's hockey.

Get the
eBook free!*
details inside
*proof of purchase
required